101

Inspirational

Stories

of the

Priesthood

101
Inspirational
Stories
of the
Priesthood

Compiled by
Sister Patricia Proctor, OSC

Foreword by
Father Darrin Connall

Inspirational Stories Edited by
Anne Marie Lillis
Cathy Felty

Cover and Illustrations by
Ted Schluenderfritz

A Called by Joy Book

Franciscan Monastery of Saint Clare
Spokane, Washington

www.calledbyjoy.com

ISBN-13: 978-0-9728447-3-3
ISBN-10: 0-9728447-3-2

Library of Congress Control Number: 2005927274

ATTENTION SCHOOLS, UNIVERSITIES, COLLEGES
AND CHARITABLE ORGANIZATIONS:
Quantity discounts are available on bulk purchases of this book for educational, gift purposes or as premiums for increasing magazine subscriptions or renewals. For information, please contact:
St. Anthony Messenger Press at 1-800-488-0488.

Dedication

to Sister Mary Rita Dolan, OSC

This book was the deep desire of our Abbess, Sister Mary Rita,
she offered the last eight weeks of her life in pain and suffering
that this book would be a blessing for our Priests and our Church.

Her words were, "If this book is all it is supposed to be,
I will be among the first to kneel down and thank God."

She went to heaven the day after the book was sent
to the printer.

This is Sister Mary Rita's book!

With Prayerful Thanks

No doubt about it—my first words of thanks definitely go to Our Blessed Mother. Without her help, this book truly would have never made it to the printer. Thank you dearest Mother!

The next big thank you goes to my community of Poor Clare Sisters. Each sister gave me unending encouragement and generously provided me with the time and space needed to see this book through to the end. Their help in selecting the stories was a great blessing that I am very thankful for. Choosing stories is never an easy task when each one we receive has a special message of love and blessings to convey. It is very difficult to pick just some of them.

The two editors of the stories, Anne Marie Lillis and Cathy Felty, must be given great applause for their masterful craftsmanship in bringing out the best in each story. They tuned them just enough to promote easy reading, and yet carefully stayed as true as possible to each author's submission.

Virginia Schmuck was the proofer par excellent! She worked on a timetable that was totally impossible, and yet did a superb job in catching all the little bloopers and twists of sentences that often happen in any written work. Truly, Anne Marie, Cathy and Virginia must be given a standing ovation for a job well done! God bless you!

Barb Ries is my true friend who continually pulled me out of every pit I seemed to fall into in getting this book ready. She is the glue that pulled things together by typing stories, filling in the data for each submission, contacting authors, etc., etc., etc. For every job that seemed to overwhelm me time and time again, she was there to pick up the slack and move us forward. Three cheers for Barb!

Then there is my other great friend, Dale Duncan. Dale is listed as "layout editor" but that was just one of the hats he donned for this book and the previous ones. Dale is the master magician who can take a collection of scattered edited stories, indexes, artwork, and other assorted jumble mumble from the far corners of the earth and turn them into a book—a book that looks great from beginning to end. Hooray for Dale!

Thank you very much to Father Darrin Connall who encouraged this book from the beginning and was always on hand for suggestions, decisions and guidance. It was a joy working with you.

Truly, this book was a team effort. A team of wonderful authors, friends and comrades who helped row when the rowing got tough, and bailed when the boat started taking on water. At times I have to admit this little boat took on a lot of water!

I know I will fall short in expressing thanks to the many people who contributed to this book. I will end, though, with thanks to Kathy Czeck and all the wonderful people at Park Press who proved that printing a book is more than just paper and a press. Their quality control and attention to every detail is stupendous!

And finally, of course, a huge thanks to Father Jeremy Harrington, OFM, and all the staff at Saint Anthony Messenger for their help and advice and especially for taking on the responsibility of full distribution of our books. Long live the Franciscans! You can find all of our books at www.americancatholic.org plus many other great reads as well.

With grateful thanks,
I ask God to bless you with All Peace and All Good!

Sister Patricia Proctor, OSC

Contents

Foreword

On November 30, 2004, I had the opportunity to celebrate Mass for the Poor Clare Sisters at their monastery in Spokane, Washington. It was the feast of St. Andrew. After Mass I was speaking with Sister Patricia Proctor, OSC, about the call of St. Andrew, his response to Jesus, and the need we have today to encourage vocations to the priesthood. We agreed that millions of people each day have powerful encounters with holy priests dedicated to the faithful service of God's people. We also agreed that those stories needed to be told. This book, *101 Inspirational Stories of the Priesthood* was born, in part, from that conversation.

In his last Holy Thursday letter to the priests of the world, Pope John Paul the Great challenged those of us who are priests to encourage vocations to the priesthood by the manner in which we live our lives.

"Vocations will certainly not be lacking if our manner of life is truly priestly, if we become more holy, more joyful, more impassioned in the exercise of our ministry. A priest 'won' by Christ more easily 'wins' others, so that they too decide to set out on the same adventure," (2005 Holy Thursday Letter to Priests).

This is a book of stories about priests who have been "won" by Christ—ordinary men whose lives are characterized by holiness, joy and a passion for ministry. These 101 stories will no doubt be an inspiration to all of God's people—renewing our reverence and love for this essential ministry in the life of the Church. My hope is that they will also be an inspiration to young men considering service to the Church as a priest. Just as St. Andrew left everything to follow Jesus two thousand years ago, may these stories inspire many young men to do the same today.

Fr. Darrin Connall
Vocation Director
Diocese of Spokane

Introduction

Every authentic Christian vocation in the Catholic Church is a work of the Holy Spirit. This is true because every baptized Catholic Christian shares in Christ's threefold mission as priest, prophet, and king. It would make sense then that every vocation is both inspired and inspiring. St. Basil in a treatise on the Holy Spirit says that "To the Spirit all creatures turn in their need for sanctification; all living things seek him according to their ability. His breath empowers each to achieve its own natural end."

Webster's defines *inspirational* with the top two points: "1: a divine influence or action on a person believed to qualify him or her to receive and communicate sacred revelation 2: the action or power of moving the intellect or emotions." I think each of the above definitions in equal measure commingle in the vocation of priesthood.

Priestly ordination is a uniquely graced sharing in Christ's threefold mission of priest, prophet and king. The power given to priests so they are able to administer the great sacraments of the Church make the vocation, and hence the experiences and stories of the priesthood special and unique. This is not because priests are better people than others in the Church. Indeed God chooses to work through weak human instruments to complete his work on earth. Priests are weak instruments. But God's graces working in less than perfect creatures makes them strong in bearing witness to Him. This is no less true of priests and the priesthood in particular.

In the Office of Readings for the feast of Pentecost, it is instructive to hear St. Irenaeus confirm that God sent His Son into the world to strengthen us in our weakness. He says in his treatise *Against Heresies*, "If we are not to be scorched and made unfruitful, we need the dew of God. Since we have our accuser, we need an Advocate as well. And so the Lord in his pity for man, who had fallen into the hands of brigands, having himself bound up his wounds and left for his care two coins bearing the royal image, entrusted him to the Holy Spirit. Now, through the Spirit, the image and inscription of the Father and the Son have been given to us, and it is our duty to use the coin committed to our charge and make it yield a rich profit for the Lord."

In our current age when we are experiencing all sorts of cultural and institutional challenges, it is important to allow ourselves to know that wonderful things are taking place in the name of Christ, by His power, and through His priesthood. We need to hear that many priests are dutifully using the coin committed to them to yield a rich harvest for the Lord. Especially in this year of the Eucharist, it is appropriate that this publication of stories about priests and priesthood is shared with the world. Christ is working in His Church. Christ is working through His priesthood. And Christ will continue to work miracles of grace and healing through weak human instruments undeserving of such an exalted calling and ministry.

Rev. William Watson, SJ
Assistant for Colombia and International Ministries
Author, Inviting God into Your Life

My Reflections on Priesthood

For me, the call to priesthood has always been a mystery. I felt a strong call to become a priest when I was about twelve years old and growing up in a very non-Catholic region of north-central Washington state. I assisted my pastor as an altar boy in two rural parishes, forty miles apart, because my family's apple farm was almost equal distance between the two parishes. Since Catholics were so few, everyone knew everyone else even though they lived some distance from one another. Eucharist brought them together, and it was the priest through his ministry who was the convener and helped to make community happen.

As I reflect back over my priesthood, especially as a bishop, I marvel at the opportunity and unusual circumstances of celebrating Eucharist that have been especially meaningful in my own life.

The regular parish visits in the diocese to celebrate sacraments, especially Eucharist, have always been enriching and inspiring. Everywhere I go in the Church, I find holy people who are faithful and deeply committed to community: the organ player; the lady who, for decades, has taken care of the linens; the man who has taken care of the parish grounds for years; and the catechist who has taught classes for thirty-five years. These are just a few instances of exemplary people living ordinary lives of generous service and commitment.

Unusual circumstances of celebrating Eucharist also come to mind. In the 1980s, when I was bishop of the Diocese of Yakima, Washington, I remember the call early one summer morning that St. Pius X Church in Quincy had burned to the ground during the night. The pastor was away on vacation, and I felt it was very important to be with the parish community for the weekend Masses. Although a local, non-Catholic faith community had generously offered their church for our use, the parishioners wanted to be near the sacred ground of their parish church, so we celebrated on the lawn in front of the burned out structure. The celebration of the Eucharist was especially one of consolation, gratitude and hope. People began talking immediately of building a new facility, and about a year later they had a beautiful new parish church.

During that same period while I was in Yakima, Circus Vargas came to town. Shortly before they arrived, the Little Sisters of the Poor, who traveled with the circus as wardrobe managers, called and requested that I celebrate the sacrament of confirmation and first Eucharist for some members of the circus troupe. They had prepared the children, and we celebrated Mass, including the sacraments of initiation, under the big tent. Later that evening, I attended the circus performance and watched with amazement as the young people, who just a few hours before were confirmed and received first Eucharist, displayed their skills, flying on the trapeze and working with the elephants.

One of the great gifts of priesthood is the universal connection we have through Eucharist in the body of Christ. On a trip to Zimbabwe and Malawi in the southern part of Africa a few years ago, there were several celebrations of Eucharist that I will always remember. The first took place even before reaching Africa, at Gatwick Airport outside of London, where we gathered in the airport chapel to celebrate Mass. The forty people present were from all over the world, drawn together for that hour as brothers and sisters to celebrate and receive the *Bread of Life*. They were, for those sixty minutes, like family, even though they had never before met each other. What a privilege to be there!

In Lilongwe, Malawi, there is a large community of Poor Clare sisters, and the bishop invited me to preside at their Eucharist. The special feast day included the singing of the "Gloria" at Mass, with the sisters beautifully waving small branches, singing in harmony, and gently dancing this prayer of praise.

A few days before, I had celebrated Mass at Simbala School near Binga Rest Camp in Zimbabwe. The school was just a very rudimentary structure with a couple of rooms, but the beauty of the liturgy in song and participation left me profoundly humbled.

A few experiences of priesthood—powerful and tremendously inspiring. How greatly blessed I have been, and I constantly need to thank God and the Church.

Bishop William S. Skylstad   *Spokane, Washington*

Gift of Joy

In our days of sadness and scandals that seem to be an evil fog lingering over our churches, I am happy to tell you about Father Treml, who was once a part of St. Margaret of Scotland Parish, which is located north of Detroit, Michigan.

St. Margaret of Scotland is a very large parish. Although I didn't know Father Treml personally, I saw the joy of his priestly vocation shine out of him like a bright morning sunrise over a fresh coating of snow. He surely had the gift of joy from the Holy Spirit.

Father Treml's enthusiasm at Mass and demeanor in the daily functions of being a priest was always upbeat and happy. This terrific priest, who went into the seminary at an older age, truly loves people and what he is doing. I have never seen a priest so happy and fulfilled in his priestly vocation.

At many Masses he lifted my spirits with his joyful smile and vibrant attitude. He usually started the celebration with the phrase "God is good!" and the congregation would respond "All the time!"

Father Treml was at St. Margaret of Scotland Parish around 2002. He has since been transferred to SS. Peter and Paul Parish in North Branch, Michigan.

Dennis J. Casnovsky   *Alma, Michigan*

A Good Priest Reaches a Thousand Lives

In 1997, I was a senior in high school in Spokane, Washington, looking for a college to attend the following year. I didn't really know what I wanted in a school, except that it needed to be an upper-tier school as far away from home as possible. I finally decided on the engineering school at the University of Pennsylvania, even though I knew little more about it than what I could glean from the brochures and through telephone conversations with admissions personnel.

Looking back, neither the school nor the major I chose were well suited to my personality. So how did I manage to stick it out for four years? The answer can be traced back to Father Chuck.

One of my first memories of college was the Freshman Retreat at the Newman Center, where Father Chuck Pfeffer was the chaplain. That experience gave me a good foundation of acquaintances at this large and very secular school—people who shared a lot of the same values as I did.

Around the middle of that first semester, Father Chuck sent out an announcement about an upcoming leadership retreat sponsored by an outside group. I was interested but was not sure if I could do it because I was struggling to prepare for midterm exams. Somehow, Father Chuck convinced me to go.

As a result, my grades were terrible, but the retreat was truly a life-changing experience. On the drive home I was feeling pretty inspired and was acting quite silly. Father Chuck just laughed along with me, but he later revealed that after seeing me that day he thought I must have been one of the *quota kids*, meaning the university had only accepted me because they needed more people from the state of Washington.

Despite this, he had recognized my excitement for campus ministry and encouraged me to get involved with the Newman Council, the student group that planned and led the activities for the Catholic student community. Two years later I became president of the group—just what I deserved for going along with Father Chuck!

I remember that during those years he was constant and mellow, filled with humor and wisdom for all of us who were struggling amidst academic and romantic ups and downs, as conflicts and politics arose within our community, and as I grieved over the deaths of three family members and one classmate. There were times when it was such a struggle that I honestly think I would have given up and transferred if it hadn't been for Father Chuck. His presence and his open ear gave me hope that at least there was one thing worth staying for at the university.

As I took on more responsibility within the Newman community, I had the privilege of spending more and more time with Father Chuck. In my junior and senior years, I would try to make a *brief stop* by his office, but it would turn into a two-hour conversation about our vision for the future of the Newman community. The theme of our discussions often revolved about the idea that we had to meet people where they were on their own faith journeys, rather than expecting them to meet us where we were—something he definitely did with me.

I appreciated how Father Chuck treated me as a peer even though I wasn't, and sometimes it caused him to be painfully honest. One of my favorite memories is after our elections, when he told me he was glad to have me as the new president but that I had completely shot myself in the foot in my speech. I already knew this, but no one else around me was going to say it. The fact that he cracked a joke about it showed he thought I could handle it and that he saw the potential in me to grow from it.

I will always cherish Father Chuck as one of the few people I knew during a difficult transition in my life. He could see the potential in me and chose to invest his time, energy, and resources into my development, both as a leader and as a person of faith. I feel very blessed to have chosen the *wrong* college and to have ended up spending the time I did with Father Chuck.

He had many health complications related to diabetes that were worsened by his inability to put his own needs before that of the community, so he ended up being away for much of my term as Newman

President. His health seemed to improve for some time, but during the winter of 2004, two years after I left Philadelphia, Father Chuck died unexpectedly in his sleep.

In the following days, it was exceedingly apparent that one of his most wonderful characteristics was his humility. Most of us at Newman had no idea how influential he had been in the greater Catholic community until we had been there a long time and started to see all the projects in which he was involved. The large and diverse crowd that turned out for his funeral on a bitterly cold day just after Christmas 2004 was a testimony to his life. Listening to all the humorous and touching stories about his life was a testament to what a difference a good priest can make in thousands of lives.

Amanda L. Spethman   *Randolph Center, Vermont*

My Close Friend and Listener

I had known my boyfriend for eight years. All seemed to be well until I got pregnant and gave birth to our daughter. We moved in together, and it was a disaster. The very first night I moved in, he was out with another woman, while my friends helped me unload the U-Haul truck. I didn't find this out right away, but I knew things were not good.

The relationship continued to go downhill. He continued to go out with his friends, drinking and using drugs, which he felt were much more fulfilling than being home with his family. It lasted for about six months. Towards the end, he stopped even coming home most nights, and I was completely alone except for my daughter, Kristina.

I was so unhappy. All I did was sit in the rocking chair with my baby girl and cry. My eyes would be full of tears as I rocked her. She would look up at me and smile as if to say, "Okay, Mom. It will be okay."

The turning point finally came when I called my sister to have someone to talk to. She thought I was having a nervous breakdown, and immediately she and her husband drove for three hours in the middle of the night to get us out of there.

Over the next few years, I tried to put the pieces of my life back together. My ex-boyfriend continued to give me a hard time. He wanted custody rights, even though he cared nothing for our daughter. At first I stayed with my brother but then moved on to the Oregon coast. At last I had the opportunity to get a job in Spokane at a Catholic Retreat Center where my aunt worked.

It was there that God opened the first major door for my healing. When I first went to work at the Retreat Center, I met Monsignor William Van Ommeren—or Father Van. At first I felt very uncomfortable around him because he seemed a little standoffish, but after a few months it became very apparent that he was the most kind and gentle person that anyone would want to know. He was just a bit shy.

Father Van became a very close friend and listener. Any time that I felt I needed someone to talk with or to give me some advice, I would go to see Father Van. Never once did he turn me away or tell me what I should do. He would listen quietly and then offer suggestions. He is one of the most gracious and loving priests that I have ever known.

I remember that once Father Van had me go to see someone at the chancery for counseling. I was there so long that I got a parking ticket. Later, when I told him about this, he asked , "Did it help you any?"

I said, "Yes, it helped a lot."

He said, "Good. Then I will pay for the ticket." And he did.

Barbara Ries   *Spokane, Washington*

Secret to Finding Time

At one point in my life, going to Mass every Saturday or Sunday seemed to be just a weekly ritual for me. I'd go to church, say some prayers (usually for the first time that week), the Mass would begin, and I would listen to the sermon. Sometimes I found myself drifting off to never-never land while the priest talked. However, this particular Saturday at St. Joan of Arc Catholic Church was different. For some reason, I felt a strong need to listen more intently. I guess it was God's way of telling me, "I'm going to fill you in on a little secret." As Father Leslie Vance began his sermon on prayer, I became engrossed in his words.

Until that point, I thought the reason I didn't pray much during the week was because I didn't have time, with work and all. Then, on that special Saturday, the secret to finding time to pray was divulged when Father Les said, "At least once a week, turn the radio off on your way to work and talk to God for a few moments." I knew then that God was sending that message to me through Father Les.

It has been about fourteen years since I heard that sermon, and to this very day I never turn the radio on when I am driving; I use that time to talk to God. I carry one decade of rosary beads in the car and always make sure I grab them and make the sign of the cross before I start the car. Then, while driving, I either pray a decade of the rosary or simply talk to God. Not only do I ask Him for favors, but I also thank Him for the things He has given me. The day of Father Les's sermon was a new beginning for me and I will always be grateful to him for bringing me back to Our Lord on a daily basis through prayer.

Lois M. Smith   *San Antonio, Texas*

A Gospel Man for Others

When I attended Gannon College in Erie, Pennsylvania, I never imagined that my life would be so profoundly changed by a priest, Monsignor Louis Lorei—Father Louis, Dean of Humanities.

Our association began with a simple meeting for schedule advice and approval. I remember his busy look turning warm and engaging.

"I'm impressed that you put 'J.M.J.' at the top of your worksheet," he said, smiling.

He took a shine to the fact that I seemed a regular guy with a keen interest in my Catholic faith. You might say our friendship started in the hearts of Jesus, Mary and Joseph—the persons those initials represented.

Shortly thereafter, I began serving at his Mass at the St. Joseph Motherhouse of Josephite Sisters in Erie, in a magnificent Victorian-Gothic style chapel. At the altar I was able to see a priest deeply in love with his eucharistic Lord and eager to communicate that love for Jesus to others. His sermons were short but packed with theological insight that always *hit home* for our modern day needs.

I was privileged to accompany him after Mass to the infirmary as he brought Communion to the aged and ill sisters. Here, too, he showed a warm compassion in his posture and tone, a genuine reverence, and love toward each sister who had given her life to Christ.

Through the Mass and these eucharistic visits our friendship was growing daily in Christ. My freshman year quickly passed and I found myself a sophomore, I was invited many times to his family farm where I was welcomed by his endearing mother and siblings. At the farm we enjoyed walks through the woods and talks at the beaver dam, and we shared heartfelt rosaries.

I was not the only beneficiary of this good man. Countless students were quietly helped by his generosity—students in trouble who needed redirection and kids who were broke and had to find cash for certain necessities. Many adults in town who were down and out were helped by Father in any way he could. All this gradually came to my knowledge through other people who knew him or received love from him.

Father Louis was a man who loved his priesthood. He saw it as an extension of Jesus' saving ministry in the Gospel. He saw his priesthood as a gift within the Church, a gift to share with others, a gift handed down from the beginning of the infant Church and received from the apostles. He was part of this holy drama, making it real and viable for contemporary people.

The period following Vatican II was a difficult time for the Church. There were extremes on both sides, a lot of confusion, and a lot of "throwing the baby out with the bath water." Father Louis was different. He maintained a steady, balanced approach, embracing the openness and freshness of Vatican II while retaining our magnificent traditions of culture and devotions, especially the great tradition of handing down the faith with the daily illumination of the spirit.

With his help I was able to stay in the wholesome middle, remain calm during the storm, and "fight the good fight" for the faith with the strength that comes from internal balance and with the guidance of a holy mentor. Sixteen years passed and our love and friendship remained steadfast—always deepening.

In 1986 I received a beautiful letter from Father describing his sense of freedom and joy in the service of the Lord and in his love for Mary. He was seeing life in new and exciting ways: a resurgence of his identity in the church as a man for others. He had been walking and running track, eating well and feeling fit, physically and spiritually.

This newness came after a period of struggle with the dark night that all spiritual hearts go through in order to become stronger in their faith and commitment. It also came after a very tough time of sudden calumny that was a real, personal *passion* for Father Louis, one he offered in union with Jesus' cross. Now, the freshness of being alive and being one with

God was apparently a beautiful preparation, it seems, for the glory that was to open up for him in his ultimate meeting with the Lord.

Only a brief time after this the Lord called him home. Father Louis died of a heart attack. The funeral was a tremendous tribute to him by the bishop, hundreds of his brother priests, and a cathedral jammed with laity and many religious congregations. The many people he had helped out over the years were also on hand.

The family asked me to be one of the pallbearers. I can't tell you the personal loss I experienced, the pain of losing a friend, a father in Christ, my special priest. He had often told me that God gave me to him to be "the son he always wanted." I remember the final moments at the old family graveyard on the farm, the farm where we had shared so much mutual faith and joy in our spiritual association.

As I walked away from the burial site, I kept thinking how the priesthood was his whole being and about how he *offered up* Mass each day with such joy and belief in the transforming power of Christ's sacrifice at Calvary and His risen love that is re-presented at the altar. I thought, too, of how he became a *living sacrifice*, as St. Paul exhorts all of us, for Christ and for those around him. That was what Father Louie did and was.

And now he is a priest forever with the Eternal High Priest, Jesus. I know he hasn't stop praying for me, or us, and the whole church: we who are still on the Gospel pilgrimage, the journey through life. I can't imagine Father Louis being satisfied with resting. Loving was always giving, in his opinion. With that other active, outreaching spiritual giant, St. Therese of the Child Jesus, Father Louis must be doing good work for us here on earth.

Jesus, Mary and Joseph, thank you for the priesthood and witness of love of Father Louis Lorei! Thank you very much!

John Joseph D. Schweska   *Green Brook, New Jersey*

The Day I Learned to Love Confession

To a child growing up in the 1960s, the Church was a mysterious and wondrous thing; it was also sometimes frightening. I received my first reconciliation in 1967 and since our school, St. Teresa's, was right beside the church, we went once a month for class confession times. On one of those occasions, I entered the confessional booth and the assistant pastor was in *the box*. I began with the usual, "Bless me father for I have sinned…"

After I recounted my sins, the priest asked me a question. I answered, but did not say, "Yes, father," at the end of my response. He rebuked me for that in a voice loud enough that my classmates (and I was convinced anyone else within one mile) could have been able to hear. I was then told, again loud enough for everyone to hear, that I had to go to the front of the church and pray a full rosary. I rushed out of the confessional with tears streaming down my face and spent the next thirty minutes on my knees, crying my way through the rosary. I continued to cry all through recess.

Time went on and my absolute dread of the sacrament of reconciliation never passed. In fact, every time I went to confession during my school years, I would break into a cold sweat while I was in line waiting for my turn. Sometimes I came very close to fainting. Needless to say, when I was no longer *forced* to go to confession because of a school requirement, I promptly stopped going.

I moved from tumultuous, temptation-filled teenage years into a very sinful young adulthood. Eventually I began attending St. Mary's Parish in Ottawa, Canada, where Father Bob Bedard was the pastor. I had a renewal of my faith in September of 1986, and my need to return to the sacrament of reconciliation fell upon me in full force. After I had put off my desperate and inevitable need to go to confession for a few months, Lent rolled around and the Lenten reconciliation service approached.

The thought of going to confession sent my heart into palpitations, and overwhelming fear and dread haunted me for days before the reconciliation service. I went to the service but was so nervous that I didn't hear anything that was said or any of the prayers that were prayed. The examination of conscience that was read was an absolute blur to me.

Finally, the time arrived for us to line up for confession. A number of priests were there and I ended up in the line for Father Bob. Waiting for my turn with my palms sweating, I hoped for a fire alarm to go off, or some kind of natural disaster to occur (hope springs eternal!). But then the moment arrived. I made my way over to the empty chair that was in front of Father Bob. He was sitting in persona Christi, waiting for me. With my legs feeling like jelly, I plopped myself down into the chair before I fell into it in a dead faint. I must have been as white as a sheet.

I began, "Bless me father, for I have sinned." I couldn't go on. Father Bob looked at me with compassion in his eyes. Then I blurted out the whole story of my bad experience from when I was seven years old, and told him how petrified I was of sitting with him now. Upon hearing the tearful conclusion of my story, Father Bob looked me right in the eyes and said, "Christine, on behalf of that priest, I ask your forgiveness for hurting you in this way."

A simple sentence, really, and yet so powerful. I have rarely felt such sweet relief in my life. In that instant, all the fear, dread, and trepidation washed right out of me. I was overcome with the tremendous sense of how much God loved me, and how much He cared about what would seem to many such a small thing. I was overcome with the peace of the Lord that surpasses all understanding.

I forgave Father Bob as he stood in for that harsh priest from so long ago, and the sweet release of the forgiveness of Jesus flowed between us. Then I went on to make my confession for the first time in twenty years. And, thanks to Father Bob's willingness to stand in the place of that priest, I was healed. I am released from a bondage that would have prevented me from experiencing the forgiving love of Jesus through the sacrament of reconciliation.

Just one caring and sincere sentence from Father Bob changed my life forever. Now I go to confession on a monthly basis so I can receive the grace of Jesus, and I continue to seek holiness in every area of my life. I will be grateful forever for this special priest who responded to the Lord's prompting. He set me free to experience the forgiving grace of our heavenly Father. Thanks so much Father Bob.

Christine M. Labrosse   *Gloucester, Ontario, Canada*

God Is Good! Amen!

My story is one of how my life was changed forever because of one of God's precious priests. I was a very *prideful, protesting Protestant,* but because of Father John Noonan I became a *crazy, charismatic Catholic.*

Father John was the assistant pastor of St. Elizabeth of Hungary Catholic Church in Pompano Beach, Florida. It was the mid-1980s; my husband was Catholic and I wasn't.

I had been raised a Baptist, but by this time I had moved into the non-denominational stage.

I knew I should be obedient to my husband, so I attended church with him and our two children. During Father John's homilies, I had trouble sitting still and had to sit on my hands to keep from raising them in praise to God for what this priest was saying. His words burned in my heart, and I wanted to shout, "Halleluiah!"

I was very anti-Catholic at the time, but I knew the truth when I heard it, and he was *preaching it like it was, Praise God!* I used to go home each Sunday and cry all afternoon because I couldn't give praise to God like I wanted to. Then my husband decided that our children should be baptized.

"Oh, no!" I thought. "If my kids are baptized Catholic, they will go to hell for sure!"

My husband asked me if I would allow the priest to come over to our house after Mass one Sunday so he could talk to me about the situation. I agreed, and Father John came over. We talked for three hours—he and I had a blast! He was so patient, loving, kind and funny. All I gave him was a drink of ice water—I never thought he would stay so long. He skipped to his car that day, and before he left, he asked me if he could return the following week. I agreed.

The next week he came again and we spent two more hours talking. He told us that he felt we should go to a local charismatic Catholic church because he knew it was Catholic and that would satisfy my husband, but he also knew I would like it because of the praise. He also said that our children would have to have Confraternity of Christian Doctrine (CCD) classes to be baptized since they were old enough to understand what was happening.

I think he must have done a lot of praying for me, too. The last thing I remember telling him was, "Both you and my husband will be six feet under before I ever become a Catholic," (I said it nicely, though!). Then we took his advice, and after several more years of *Protestant procrastination*, I finally started taking Rite of Christian Initiation of Adult (RCIA) classes.

During this time, I was the founder of the Sonlight Clown Ministry at our church, San Isidro Catholic Church in Pompano Beach, and we were going to put on a program during one of our monthly revivals. I wondered how I could get in touch with Father John so I could invite him and thank him. Several years had passed and he was no longer at St. Elizabeth's. At this time I did not know about being able to contact the Archdiocese to find a priest.

I am also a registered nurse working in outpatient surgery, and when I went to work the next day and walked past a patient lying on a stretcher, I did a double take. It was Father John. I had asked God for his address and He gave me Father John in the flesh.

I had not seen him for years, so I wasn't sure if he would remember me—but he did. And when I told him the story of wanting to contact him, but not knowing how, the hair on our arms stood up as we realized God had arranged our meeting. He was very pleased to hear that I was in the RCIA class and becoming a Catholic. It was all because of Father John's patience and love that I became a Catholic. I entered the Catholic Church at the Easter Vigil, 1991.

God has continued to place Father in our lives at the most surprising times. Both of our children also became Catholic, and when our son was being confirmed I saw the bishop and a priest go down the aisle—was that Father John? It was! After Mass I told him that my son was the "fruit of his ministry," as it was because of him that my son was baptized and confirmed. He then told me that he was not supposed to be there that night; the other priest had gotten ill and he was asked to fill in at the last moment.

Father John is now a monsignor and is currently the president/rector of our seminary, St. John Vianney College Seminary in Miami. My husband and I have a ministry for priests, but that is a long story of God's mercy and His grace. I continue to give God all the glory. God is good, all the time! Amen!

Lesley M. Vaitekunas   *Coconut Creek, Florida*

A Miracle of God's Grace

I was raised a cradle Protestant and imbibed the usual prejudices against Catholics that most serious Protestant Evangelicals have. Therefore I can honestly say it took a miracle of God's grace, with help from a very holy priest, to bring me to the true faith.

In 1995, at thirty-three years old, with five children—including six-month-old twins—I found myself facing a move to Randolph, a small town in central Vermont, on a *call* from our church to establish a *mission.*

My husband and I had been part of a small, independent evangelical church for at least a decade. We had built a church school and even a church co-op, and the next logical step seemed to be to expand the base of operations by sending two or three families out as *seed churches* to other communities. We volunteered to go, never dreaming of the dramatic change it would begin in our lives.

A few years earlier, while browsing a local library sale, I had come across a very old book called *The Little Flower* that contained the autobiography of St. Therese of Lisieux. As I read it, I was faced with an insoluble question. Either St. Therese was *saved* despite being Catholic, or she was able to serve Our Lord, to be a true *Christian* because of the Roman Catholic Church.

Questions on the role of Mary, of Jesus truly present in the Eucharist, and of there being one, true Church began to haunt me and made me think. I found other Catholic books, especially the lives of the saints, and almost literally devoured them. I found much grace and wisdom in them, and a sense of peace I hadn't found in other evangelical sources.

I also found the strange allure of truth in the books I read. Our church, like most Protestant and evangelically oriented churches, was constantly looking for truth. We had changed in the years I had been attending from a Calvinistic to a Reformed to a semi-Anglican viewpoint in matters of salvation history. That made it difficult to think clearly and logically about God and His ways of dealing with His people. I often found myself hard-pressed when faced with questions about Christianity beyond, "Why you need to know Jesus."

With the stress and loneliness of moving from a very integrated community to a new, unfamiliar town, these questions began to become insistent in me. I had discussed this with my husband many times, and while he did not feel the attraction to Catholicism that I did, he did realize the problems our church was having with doctrine and a clear grasp on truth. In the meantime, he had become an elder of the church and often led the Sunday worship, preaching and distributing communion. This presented me with quite a conflict and I often would pray to the Lord to give me a good, strong (Protestant!) faith and remove my doubts.

I was now about five years older and one afternoon, while I was walking into the local bank, a man ahead of me waited and held the door open. Absorbed in my own interests, I barely looked up to say, "Thank you, sir…uh, Father." It was the local priest! I had never seen him before, although, since it was a small town, I had heard his name, Father John Milanese, mentioned. With a smile and a nod, he went to his banking business and I to mine. The ladies at the bank greeted him cheerfully and while trying to keep my mind on my own business, I worked hard at overhearing every word they exchanged. I personally had never spoken to a priest before in my life.

A new idea entered my head after that day. Perhaps I should attend a Mass at SS. Donatian and Rogatian Church, and then, after seeing it was no different from any other church service, I could go back to a nice, quiet life without all these doubts and questions assailing me. I could sneak into Mass on a Saturday evening and no one of our circle would be the wiser. It took a few months to screw up my courage, but after receiving my husband's permission, one Saturday I walked into our small Catholic church. I was absolutely petrified. But there I was and I was determined to stick it out and take care of this once and for all.

Well, I got through the opening prayer and was rather scandalized when there was a woman lector. Well, I thought, this isn't very special. I believe even the deacon spoke that week and it wasn't a very impressive sermon for someone who'd heard probably more than her share of sermons. I was aware of a feeling of mingled relief with disappointment.

Then, however, the priest I'd seen in the bank rose and the consecration began. He celebrated so reverently, with such heartfelt devotion, that when he genuflected before the Host, the thought "He really believes this! He really believes that is Jesus!" seared through my mind. When the priest elevated Our Lord and said, "Behold the Lamb of God", I found myself saying, "My Lord and my God!"

Although I had never exchanged a word with him, the conduct of Father John while saying Mass told me the most essential things about him. When we met with him to speak about me entering the Church, my husband decided to begin instruction to become Catholic also.

In the months, and now years, that have passed, he has grown more and more dear to my family and me. Father John Milanese is a true man of God, a true son of Mary and a true *alter Christus.* May God bless him and draw him always close to His heart.

Elizabeth A. Mahaffy   *East Randolph, Vermont*

You're Going To Hell

I was the first child of six, born to two very young and unstable people. As a child, I spent a lot of time at the Catholic school on the north side of Chicago where my two brothers, three sisters, and I were enrolled. It was a consistent, stable, safe place.

Home was another matter. My father was known to beat us for the slightest provocation—for misbehaviors and mistakes as real and imagined by him. Although he was a lapsed Catholic at the time, he made pronouncements on Church law as if he were the pope himself. I had no reason not to believe him, after all, he was my father. My mother claimed she could not interfere with this abuse.

In the spring of third grade, one of us girls left a jump rope on the floor. Each of us had received the same style of jump rope for Easter, and our initials were marked inside the plastic handle. I knew I had not played with mine when my father went on a rampage regarding the mislaid toy. It was a small thing. I told him it wasn't mine.

My mother came into the room and told him to look at the initials inside the plastic handle. One of my sisters must have used my jump rope and mislaid it because it turned out indeed to be mine.

This was all it took to set Daddy off on a tangent. After being yanked by the hair and beaten with a belt I was told, "You're a liar, you know that? You're nothing but a liar, and you're going to hell. Yes, you are. Ask at school. You are going to hell because you just committed a mortal sin. Lying to your father is one of the biggest mortal sins that could ever happen. You're going to hell. Don't expect any priest to ever give you forgiveness."

I was devastated. I loved Jesus with all my heart, and although I wasn't overtly pious like my sister who wanted to be a nun, I did have a devotion to the Blessed Mother. I was nine years old. Childish logic conjectured that parents wouldn't intentionally lie to their children. Therefore, all I had in life was this life, then an eternity in hell.

I never considered going to confession to tell my *sin*. I was too ashamed. "The priests at church wouldn't understand," I thought. "Monsignor certainly wouldn't understand. He yelled at the big boys who didn't behave at Mass, even in the middle of the consecration." I went through the other four priests in my head. If I could be sure I would get Father Doyle, he would understand. But I couldn't be sure. The priests did not label their confessionals at the time.

I was sure that my own father knew I was going to hell and that no priest would pronounce absolution. Why even bother going to confession? Better to keep it a secret and wait it out until I was dead. Again, in childish logic, I figured that would be about the time I was forty-four years old. It would be the turn of the twenty-first century, after all.

For the next four years I avoided both confession and Communion. I was confirmed in fourth grade, convinced in my mind that I had committed yet another mortal sin by not reconciling myself before receiving such an important sacrament.

I managed to ditch confession in school by letting others go ahead of me, and then I would leave the line to use the rest room. When I returned, I would walk back to a pew as if I were ready to perform my penance. I used the excuse of breaking the fast to avoid going to Communion.

My mother asked me about it once because my sister had noticed I wasn't receiving Communion and told her (neither of my parents went to Mass with us children). I told her I was unworthy, but could never bring myself to tell her the truth. I got a lecture about how none of us is worthy.

When I was in seventh grade, it was my friend Terri who finally found out what had happened to me. She insisted that we go to confession a little early the next Saturday so we could stake out which priest went into which confessional. Then I could tell Father Doyle my problem, or as Terri put it, my "un-sin."

We spotted Father Doyle and got in his line. Terri would not let me get out of line. I closed the door when my turn came. It took me a long time to even thrust the "Bless me, Father" out of my mouth. I finally choked it out. I was sobbing.

This kind priest did not rage. He did not laugh (I did, years later, after some therapy). He was angry, but at my father, not me. He told me I had not sinned that day. His voice had an edge when he told me, "If you want me to explain it to your dad, I will. But you have the right to the seal of the confessional and privacy, just as anybody else." He then gently helped me examine my conscience and gave me absolution. My only penance was to do something nice for myself.

Terri is in heaven, having died in an accident. My father is still alive, still a bit off in his thought process. I have no idea where Father Doyle went after St. Greg. Wherever he is, he has my prayers and gratitude every day, especially at Mass when I receive Our Lord in the Eucharist with a clean conscience from regular confession.

Loretta M. Trentanelli   *Aurora, Illinois*

A Peaceful Anointing

As my husband lay dying from multiple myeloma at the age of fifty-eight, God granted us many wonderful miracles.

Dan entered hospice care on July 15, 2004, and the hospice worker expected that Dan would die very quickly by slipping into a coma and simply slipping away from us very peacefully. That was not to be. Dan rallied very unexpectedly, and for four wonderful days, many of our friends and family were able to come and say goodbye to him. There was a bit of hope that maybe, just maybe, he would survive this crisis.

During this rally, my parish priest, Father Peter Nosbush, of Holy Rosary Catholic Church in North Mankato, Minnesota, and I had many conversations about Dan and the spiritual help that both of us needed at this time. Father Peter, in his kindness and willingness to minister to both of us, offered to come to our home and anoint both Dan and me.

I knew it would be important to talk with Dan about this because Dan was not a Catholic, but was, instead, a very conservative German Methodist. I did not know if he would be receptive to this idea of anointing.

As our friends and family went in and out of the house to say goodbye, I found that I had no time to speak with Dan privately about this kind offer from Father Peter. I finally decided to say a quick prayer and hope that Dan would be receptive to Father Peter's offer. Dan enjoyed talking with Father Peter, so I took a leap of faith and called him. Father Peter offered to come over that afternoon.

Our home was full of friends when Father Peter arrived. Our children, Father Peter, and I went into the room where Dan was resting. I told Dan that Father Peter was here to anoint us.

Dan smiled and said, "That would be nice," but he did warn Father Peter that he might fall asleep.

Father Peter told him that this was all right, explaining to Dan that he didn't need to be awake for the anointing.

Dan smiled and closed his eyes. When Father Peter began the anointing, he told Dan that the Catholic prayers were just for him, and, again Dan smiled. Father Peter completed the ritual of anointing for both Dan and me. I felt very peaceful.

Dan smiled and said, "That really was nice," and then went to sleep for a while.

Dan survived for ten days in hospice care. Throughout it all, Father Peter stood with us. He called and prayed for us. Dan died as I had prayed that he would. We were with him at home. He was at peace with God. Father Peter played a great roll in that, and I will be forever grateful for his kindness to both of us.

Mallory A. Hoffman   *North Mankato, Minnesota*

Healed of a Hidden Sorrow

I was baptized a Catholic, but a great sadness happened in my life when I was eighteen years old. The event caused me to carry a very heavy burden that affected my life and relationships. I felt isolated and alone bearing my hidden sorrow.

Then one day a friend said I should accompany her to a healing Mass. I went along, and a priest with gifts of healing and discernment prayed over me. He knew nothing of me, but he opened his eyes, held my shoulders tightly and said, "You are innocent, you were just a child."

His words shook me to the core, because I knew in that instant that what he was saying was true.

I have now come to terms with my past and work for two priests, one of whom works in the healing movement. I am a personal assistant to both, and with my training as a secretary, I help them write books. One has already been published. I love my work and feel truly appreciated, respected and cared for. I am never taken for granted, and I'm even prayed for every day—how many employees can say that?

I feel deeply that the world should know just how truly good and holy many, many priests are. My earthly father died, but the Lord really has given me two fathers, the kindest, most sincere people I know.

Fiona M. Owen   *Merseyside, England*

Shower Curtain Confession

I am the youngest of eight children born to devout Catholic parents of German descent. My background was firmly rooted in the Catholic faith. However, during my college years, I wandered from my faith and was introduced to the ideas of Eastern New Age mysticism.

Although my high-school sweetheart and I were married in my hometown Catholic church, we both shunned weekly attendance at Mass until our children were old enough to receive the sacraments. When we returned to our Catholic faith, we began teaching CCD classes at our parish. During this time, I kept up with my Eastern New Age interests, reading more and more about reincarnation and other strange beliefs. I surrounded myself with New Age literature, and kept notebooks full of handwritten information.

In the fall of 1989, I found myself at a *Cursillo* retreat weekend. During the first evening of our retreat, we were told that several priests were there to hear our confessions. I sat frozen in my seat. It had been at least ten years since I had received the sacrament of reconciliation. Since beginning my quest in the New Age movement, I felt that I had no need for confession. But that night, I felt obligated to go through the motions. After all, I was sitting in the front seat of the chapel.

The retreat was located in an ancient YMCA building, and as I entered the *confessional*, I discovered that the priest was behind a faded shower curtain, sitting in the shower! I cleared my throat and he said, "Yes, child, I am here." I giggled, and then burst into tears.

After the priest gently asked me if it would be okay, he came from behind those ridiculous plastic curtains. I poured out ten years of garbage to him, and can vividly recall the kindness in his deep blue eyes that reminded me of my own father's eyes. I told him everything about my

New Age reading and notebooks, and he patiently waited and listened. He encouraged me, consoled me, counseled me, and most importantly, forgave me in the most beautiful of sacraments. I was cleansed.

This *Cursillo* retreat weekend was a great blessing, beginning with my confession. My confessor gave some of the talks during the retreat, and I learned that he and his brother had come from Slovakia in the 1930s, and both of them had become priests. Their country had been swallowed up by the Soviets, and he had endured the pain of being separated from his family and country. He spoke eloquently of loving the sacraments, and his personal testimony was powerful.

When I left the retreat, I was renewed, and I resolved to start afresh with my precious Catholic faith. I began by removing over one hundred pieces of dangerous literature from my home. My husband and I took RCIA classes at our parish, and we became re-acquainted with our beautiful Catholic faith.

Last year, our diocese ordained a new bishop and we attended the ceremony. As we were walking down a long hall to the entrance, I glanced next to me, and there was the Slovakian priest from that life-changing *Cursillo* retreat! Without missing a step, I asked if I could walk with him for a minute.

As we talked, I reminded him of the retreat and shared how he had completely turned my life around. His blue eyes sparkled as he politely smiled, listened intently, and laughed at remembering the shower curtain. Then he gave me his priestly blessing right there in the hallway.

I often think about the priest from Slovakia and what a signpost he was in my life. And I also think about that ridiculous shower curtain, and how the Lord met me in that dingy little room. I am forever grateful for that special priest, for that beautiful *Cursillo* weekend, and especially for the rich and treasured faith I now share with my husband, my children, and my four loving grandchildren. All of us are vibrantly Catholic, and a month does not go by that I don't go to confession.

I love my Catholic faith, and have a deep respect and love for all of our priests. Every one of them is precious and needed today. Thank you, Lord, for the gift of the priesthood. Keep all priests safe. Let them know they are loved. Bless them and give them courage and strength. Amen, alleluia!

Mary Joan McCarthy   *Pequot Lakes, Minnesota*

I Had No Intention of Becoming Catholic

My story begins in 1968 when I had just started working in the record room at Bibb County Department of Family and Children Services in Macon, Georgia. One day, Father Thomas Healy, the associate pastor of nearby St. Joseph's Church, toured our facility. He was the first priest I had ever met. At that time, I was a lapsed Southern Baptist and was not going to any church. And I personally had no intentions of becoming a Catholic.

Father Thomas had a happiness about him that was very contagious. After you met him once, you wanted to see him again. I was so impressed with this dark-haired Irish priest that I sent him a letter saying how much I enjoyed meeting him, and what a blessing he was.

Not long after I sent the letter, I was called to the front desk. Another very nice priest, Father Fiero, had come to see me. He was the pastor of Holy Spirit Church that was also in Macon, Georgia, and had brought some religious items for me: rosaries and all those little trinkets Catholics have. As it turned out, I had sent my letter to the wrong church!

Since I had mistakenly sent the letter to Holy Spirit Church instead of St. Joseph's, Father Fiero said he would give the letter to Father Healy. This was the only time I met Father Fiero. Tragically, he was later killed in an automobile accident. This great priest had a tight bond of friendship with the Macon firefighters because he had always followed them to fires, and all of them came to his funeral Mass at St. Joseph's Church.

When Father Healy received my letter, he invited me to attend the Catholic information classes he was having at his parish. He assured me there was no obligation to join the Catholic Church, so I went. After the courses were over, he asked me if I would like to join the Catholic Church, and needless to say, I told him that yes, I did. That was in 1969, nearly thirty-six years ago, and I have been going to St. Joseph's ever since.

Father Healy became a good friend, one you want to keep around and never let go. I'll never forget when I moved into my first apartment and Father Healy loaned me money to help with my move. And I will always remember the time my great-grandmother, who was a Southern Baptist, was in the hospital and Father Healy visited her. She told me that when he arrived, all the aides and nurses disappeared. She said they must have thought she was going to die!

St. Joseph's has had several priests that have come and gone since I first met Father Healy, but there has never been another one like him. He has an unmatched zest for life and love of Our Lord, Jesus.

Father Healy is now the pastor of a church in Germany. Last year when our current pastor, Father Cuddy, was made a monsignor at St. Joseph's Church, Father Healy came all the way from Europe to be at the installation. It had been years since I had seen him, and it was easy to see that he is still as much in love with Our Lord as he always was. He still had that same joyful smile and those laughing eyes. Nobody who has ever met Father Healy has ever forgotten him. He may be older, but he is as happy being a priest now as he was when he was younger.

So you can say that two priests have made a deep impression on my life: Father Healy and Father Fiero. God does work in mysterious ways. I believe that wherever you are in your life, you are meant to be there. I was meant to be in the record room the day Father Healy came through on his tour of the Department of Family and Children's Services.

Robby L. Strozier   *Macon, Georgia*

A Loving Heart

Father Maurice Ptacek became pastor of Our Lady of Perpetual Help in Concordia, Kansas, in July of 1981. He was the most loving and patient priest I have ever known. Even though he suffered from diabetes and had to travel fifty miles to have dialysis three times a week, this dedicated priest never let his illness interfere with his obligations. He took his duties very seriously, and even said Mass while sitting down when he was too weak from dialysis to stand.

The young people in our parish loved Father Ptacek, and he had a tremendous influence on them. He always made sure he was available on Tuesday and Wednesday nights for CCD classes where the children would run to see him. I also remember when he would step out on the altar during Mass and ask, "Are there any servers?" The boys, including my son, would literally race to be first. They couldn't wait to serve for him. He truly loved all of the children, and they always looked forward to his hugs. During his trips to receive dialysis treatments he always talked about the love he had for the children.

When my brother was going through a divorce, Father Ptacek was a great help to me personally. The bitterness I felt was consuming me. He made me see, through talking with him and through confession, that it was wrong, and that I had to turn my trust over to God.

This loving priest always found good in everything and everyone. He always had a smile, even when he was very weak and not feeling well. Some say he was too easygoing, but his gentle ways kept his Masses full on Sundays. Father Ptacek passed away in August of 1990 at the young age of sixty. To this day, people, including myself, miss him dearly. I know he helped me become stronger in my Catholic faith by his example and unselfishness.

Janice Strait   *Salina, Kansas*

Our God Is an Awesome God

Our God is an awesome God who works wonders and miracles with His wisdom, power and love. To Him be glory, honor, and praise.

I am Rev. Father Noel Morales, a Filipino born in Manila. I was raised Catholic by my parents, and was the third youngest of ten children—five boys and five girls. As a child, I was always prayerful. Oh, how I loved to hear teachings about Jesus and God. I can even remember being reprimanded once by my parents when they found out I had attended a Jehovah's Witness meeting. What can I say? I didn't know it was wrong—I was only six years old! Since I loved Jesus, I attended catechism classes until I had completed preparation and received my first Communion.

I was nine years old when my family moved to a suburban area of Manila. After I graduated from high school, I did not know what courses to take in college, so I decided to study a vocational course. When I finished it, I sent an application to Philippine Airlines. Luckily, I was hired.

However, like air, the influence of bad people is everywhere. Drug users, alcoholics, gamblers, and men of different vices are commonly found everywhere, and workplaces and offices are no exception. The department I worked in was exactly one of those environments. Employees always went out after work to have some fun, hang out in bars, and to take part in unwholesome entertainment. Since I was still young and inexperienced, and filled with sheer curiosity, I was easily convinced to go with them. And so I became one of them in everything they did.

In spite of the fact that I indeed acquired such vices, at first I was still aware that I needed to save for my future since I had plans and ambitions. My dream had always been to raise a family of my own, and I wanted to be a responsible husband to my wife and a good father to my children. Little did I know my dream was slowly drifting away.

My lack of awareness and the gradual changes in my life shifted my attention away from my future goals. I did not realize I was falling away from God. I stopped going to church on Sundays and on my birthdays as well. I didn't care about religion anymore because I had emerged into a very worldly lifestyle. I neglected my family and myself. I had long hair and a beard, and didn't bother to live a decent life. My concerns were only about personal satisfactions and worldly pleasures, which became the treasures of my heart for years.

The situation grew worse when a new guy, who was a notoriously vicious person, came to work in our department and became my close buddy. We hung out even more often than usual after work until I was completely hooked on that sinful lifestyle. I was without a right direction and was totally lost. I found I couldn't quit living that way because I was enslaved by it. It was too late for me to stop; I was helpless and had no strength. My bank account went down to a zero balance and I ran out of money. It was the darkest hour of my life.

One day I came to my senses and thought to myself, "After all these years with my life in dissipation and consumed with worldly pleasures, something is still lacking in my life." I finally realized that those temporary satisfactions and pleasures could not fill what my heart was yearning for. I asked myself once, then twice, then three times, "Why? What am I living for? Who am I?" Those thoughts kept haunting and bugging me. "Who can I turn to?" I wondered.

That evening, I found myself on my knees in prayer with tears rolling down my face as I begged God for help. That silent conversation with Him was a sort of relief and alleviation of the excruciating pains I was experiencing. It made me believe that I already had the strength I needed to finally release the burdens I carried inside myself. My relief lasted only a very short time though. As the days went on, I returned to being on my own again, back to living in my usual sinful way, yet hoping that one day God would listen to my pleas and heal me. He seemed silent, like He did not hear me.

Meanwhile, I didn't know that God was already busy working in my life. A few days later He gave me a very big surprise when His spirit led me to a person who told me about the *Cursillo* movement. God is really so good. The greatness of His love is immeasurable.

On February 14, 1980, I was sponsored by a friend and became a candidate for a *Cursillo* retreat. During that weekend retreat, something good happened. God touched me. I repented, asking forgiveness for all the sins and neglects of my life. He forgave me, changed my heart, and enlightened my mind. He mended my ways to walk in His ways, and I was completely converted. I finally fully realized my duties and responsibilities to God, my loved ones, my friends, and other people. God really does work mysteriously.

That is not the end of my story. I knew something much greater happened that retreat weekend when, two weeks later, I felt deeply troubled. Something in my mind kept bugging me. I had sleepless nights and could not get away from my thoughts. Finally I found peace of mind when I said "yes" and decided to go to my pastor to inquire about something.

It was then that God called me to a most precious gift—a vocation to the priesthood. He invited me to be His instrument, to spread His love, which is the greatest gift to mankind. This realization was the best thing that ever happened to me. I filed my resignation from Philippine Airlines Company, left my loved ones, my relatives and friends, and entered the seminary.

In June 1980 I started my first year of formation at St. Peter's College Seminary in San Pablo, and in 1985 I finished four years of AB Philosophy. That same year I joined the Missionaries of Faith and went to Italy to complete my theology requirements. I was ordained a priest in St. Peter's Basilica, Vatican City in 1991.

Right after my ordination, I went back to the Philippines to begin my ministry. I was assigned as pastor to the provincial parish, and at the same time became one of the formators of the seminarians for two years. A few years later I was given a new assignment and went to Manila, which was still an archdiocese then.

In 1998 I immigrated to the United States to continue my ministry wherever God called me. First, I worked in a parish as an associate pastor for five years. Then, in 2002, God granted me the opportunity to experience the hospital ministry, which I loved and found very rewarding and fruitful. My work as a chaplain lasted only two years, and now I'm back into parish work again. I have nothing to complain about; I live and serve God, following the will of the Lord who called me to serve Him, and who sends me wherever He needs me.

Man proposes but God disposes, "…Nor is the way of man in his own hands" (Jr. 10:23). Long ago I proposed to the Lord that I wanted to have a family of my own, but God did not dispose it. Therefore, I would rather follow His ways, not mine. After all, His ways are always the best.

Manuel A. Morales   *Suffern, New York*

Incredible Influences

Father Richard Sedlacek, Bishop William Skylstad, and the entire monastic community at St. Martin's College had an incredible influence on my life. They may not be aware of it, but each of them brought me closer to the faith and to the Catholic Church in his own unique way.

One day in the mid-1980s, Father Richard and Bishop Skylstad advised me to return to college. We were sitting at a table in a dining hall at a retreat house in Cowichee, Washington, when we had this life-changing discussion. Leonard and Char Reil were having one of their fabulous young singles retreats, and the two priests were there to minister to the young retreatants.

Both of these holy men knew my parents and were familiar with my family circumstances. We were discussing a recent large inheritance that I had received, and I was talking to them about all of my options. At age twenty-three, the choices were overwhelming. However, very early into our conversation it became clear to me that to abandon my dental assisting career in favor of returning to school for a degree in education would not be a waste of time or money.

As I look back now, I can see that it was through the grace of Almighty God that Father Richard and Bishop Skylstad were at that retreat. Their advice led me back to St. Martin's College and eventually to a degree in education. I doubt that I could have made such a drastic decision on my own.

The monastic community at St. Martin's was my greatest inspiration while I was a student there. Some of the priests and brothers were my professors, and I got to know many of them personally because they often passed through the campus information center where I worked. Many of them were always available to students for conversation and consultation.

Especially dear to me were Father George Sidel, Brother Ronald Hurst, Father Alfred, Father Kilian Malvey, Brother Ramon Newell, Father Philip Bagan, Father John Scott, Brother Aelred Woodard, and Father Conrad Raush. Brother Boniface Lazzari, Abbot Niel Roth and Father Gerard Kirsh (I'm not sure of his last name) were also a great part of student life for many students, including myself.

These special priests were always bright points in my day. They were filled with optimism and were intellectually challenging and wonderfully human. They each took a sincere interest in the personal concerns of the students, including their academic and spiritual lives. Because of their influence, I was literally drawn to the abbey church and went to daily Mass as often as possible.

My experience at St. Martin's was more than a college education.

I began to see the true human side of many priests who were very open about their lives. But most importantly I made a smooth transition in my life that seems to be very difficult for many young people: the transition of building a bridge of faith from the religion of one's youth to the Catholicism of adulthood. Because of these very blessed men, there was no gap for me. I do not think my college experience would have been as blessed and successful if not for them. To this day, my heart longs for St. Martin's, for it has become my spiritual home.

Cece Meyers   *Pomeroy, Washington*

Grandpa's Return

In the fall of 2000, my husband and I were thrilled when my father-in-law, Dick, began visiting us regularly at our lake home. He had been estranged from his family for many years, and during that time our children only saw Grandpa on holidays. For those infrequent visits we often had to find him at his workplace. One Christmas we even visited him in the boiler room of the parochial school where he was the custodian!

Our home in Pequot Lakes was within walking distance of Dick's parents' summer home on the Whitefish Chain of Lakes in northern Minnesota. Dick loved to fish, so one day we planned an afternoon out on the lake. It was hard not to notice his loss of weight and his weakness. It was obvious that his cancer had returned. We drove down to the shore to help him into the boat, and as we anchored in the cove and settled into the ritual of readying our poles, Dick made several references about ending his illness and life. In the warm Indian summer sun, we grew ever more anxious about him.

Later that day I went to see our pastor, Father George Zeck, in his office at St. Alice Parish. He listened and we prayed, and then he told me to bring Dick to daily Mass the next morning. As we sat at dinner that night my husband and I spoke frankly with Dick about our concerns. He seemed relieved.

When morning came, off we went to church. After Mass Father George quietly invited us into the sacristy. He sat Dick down and spoke softly to him; then he laid hands on Dick's head and prayed a very touching and beautiful prayer over him. He looked straight into his eyes and said, "Dick, I have heard many confessions and have seen good and bad in people's eyes. I see only good when I look into yours." Dick seemed to melt right then and there.

As we left the sacristy, my father-in-law exclaimed, "I love Father George! Can we go out to breakfast with him?" A transformational healing had occurred. Father George had not known that prior to their meeting Dick had convinced himself that he was bound for hell because of his past life. Father George had given him the greatest gift—that of hope.

Several weeks later we received a phone call from Dick. He was crying, but he assured us they were tears of joy. He told us that Father John from St. Elizabeth Ann Seton Parish in Hastings, Minnesota, had come to visit him at home. That in itself was incredible because Dick was living in the basement of his home and the only entrance was through a lower-level garage.

Father John had been told of Dick's illness. As they sat together in the dingy basement, Dick told the priest about his life. He revealed events from his past, remembering them with acute accuracy and detail. He began to cry and told Father John, "I have not gone to confession since I left for World War II when I was seventeen." Father John replied, "You have just told me your confession and now I will absolve you of your sins."

Father John told him the Bible story of the Prodigal Son. When Dick called us, he couldn't believe the forgiveness and mercy that God had given him. Soon after his confession Dick began receiving daily Communion from a dear eucharistic minister. His health was failing rapidly and he could hardly wait for Tony to visit each day with Our Lord. When he arrived, Dick would exclaim, "Did you bring my friend?"

My husband and I were blessed with spending several days with Dick as he prepared to go *home*. We witnessed a night of darkness and triumph over evil as we prayed through the night in Psalms and with the Chaplet of Mercy. At Dick's funeral, my husband spoke of God's great mercy and forgiveness. We had seen a transformation in Dick, brought about through Father George and Father John. We rejoice in the hope of being reunited with Dick one day. Dear Lord, bless our priests who bring hope, peace and rest to the penitent. Thank you for your great mercy and forgiveness. We are forever grateful. Amen.

Mary Joan McCarthy   *Pequot Lakes, Minnesota*

Growing in My Love of Christ

In putting a story together of priests who have influenced my life, it is impossible to mention only one priest. As I think of all the priests that have had an affect on my life, my earliest recollections go back to my early childhood, with my memories of Latin Mass and just trying to understand what was going on. My mother would pray her rosary while the priest, with his back to us, was bringing Jesus to us. I had no clue what was going on but just knew that it was something very special.

After I married I stopped going to church, but when my mother passed away, I started searching for God. I knew that I needed something more, since Mom had been my best friend. I church-hopped, trying to find a priest who would help fill the hole left by her passing.

I finally settled into a parish about fifteen minutes from home where we met Father Matt. Father Matt was the first priest whom I felt was a human being as well as a spiritual person. His homilies said something. He talked about God and the life we would have when we died and, in that hope, he helped me deal with my mother's death. I finally started going back to church.

When Father Mike came to our own parish a few years later, I could tell he was a man of God. He was a small person in stature with a very quiet way about him, and he gave very short and to-the-point homilies. To this day, Father Mike is still one of my favorite priests. He has since moved on to a parish a few more miles away, but I continue to attend his Masses and see him frequently because of his quiet, unassuming way. He has been there for our family more than any other priest. A few years ago, our daughter committed suicide, and from the time Father Mike heard, he was right there for us. He is still there for us, even today, though the pain of her death has dimmed.

When Father Mike was transferred away from our parish, Father Czeslaw came into my life. He was very different from Father Mike, having come to us after having taught in a seminary. Father Czeslaw is extremely intelligent and has a great love of the Bible. He always stresses this love in his homilies. He also has a great love of traditions, particularly of his Polish background, and that also shows in his homilies.

I now work in the parish of Father Art and attend his morning Mass where each day in his homily he challenges us to live like Christ. He has a great musical talent and that also shows his love of Christ and the people he serves.

Each of these priests has continued to challenge me in my love of Christ and to help me to grow in that love, and for that I thank them all.

Nancy A. Gregor   *East Aurora, New York*

My Favorite Priest

Father Daniel Rocco of St. Jude's Church in Blackwood, New Jersey, is my favorite priest. When you talk to him, he looks you straight in the eye and you know he is listening. In his homilies he translates the Gospel into present-day meaning, and I leave Mass thinking about his words and how they affect my life.

This dedicated priest visited my husband many times in the hospital, and he has helped both of us through this difficult time. His gentle compassion helps me to carry my cross. Now I have hope that I never had before. I had built a wall around myself and he taught me how to tear it down and trust again. I only wish everyone could meet and know him.

Margie Helman   *Clementon, New Jersey*

Communion in the Church Corner

The day before Christmas Eve, 2004, I had to make an early and important presentation to a group of board members for the non-profit organization where I work. Normally, my routine includes daily Mass at a church just down the street from my workplace. I was pretty nervous about the presentation and even more disturbed by the fact that giving it meant that I was going to miss Mass that morning. If ever I needed the help of the sacrament, it was that morning! I managed to arrive very early at the church so I could at least pray and spend some time before our Lord before Mass began.

Soon people began arriving and I got up to leave. As I was leaving the church, I ran into the priest who was going to say the Mass.

"Is church over already?" he asked. He laughed, but wore a quizzical look on his face because I was going in the wrong direction. I explained that I had a meeting and couldn't attend Mass.

Immediately, Father became serious and asked, "But would you like to receive Communion?" I responded with an enthusiastic, "Yes!" He told me to meet him at the altar.

My heart positively soared and my nerves immediately settled. The moments that I shared with that priest receiving Christ in the corner of that church were so precious and awesome! I am so grateful for his example, for he is very serious in his role as shepherd to the flock. A shepherd feeds his sheep, and I was truly in need.

This shepherd is Monsignor John McGraw. At the time of the incident I didn't even know his name, but I have since learned it so that I may share it with others. Although he is retired, he still says morning Mass at St. John the Evangelist Church and is truly an inspiration.

Anne M. Costa   *Baldwinsville, New York*

Something Good Is Going to Happen

"You know, for most of us, prayer is just worrying on our knees." With these words, Monsignor George A. Husmann reflected on his basic philosophy of life: that people should turn their cares over to God and learn to trust Him. If a man followed these words, he would be perfectly happy. Needless to say, that advice is what Monsignor followed every day of his life.

Born in 1916 in the small town of Fowler, Kansas, which is located in the southwestern part of the state, Monsignor Husmann was ordained a priest in 1942. Later he was raised to the rank of private chamberlain and given the title of very reverend monsignor by Pope John XXIII. In 1964, Pope Paul VI gave him the title of domestic prelate, and the title of right reverend monsignor. He served as a National Guard chaplain and as pastor in parishes in Alaska and Kansas.

In 1984, when Monsignor arrived at St. Helen Parish in Hugoton, Kansas, many of us church members were not quite sure what to expect from a man with such a high ranking title. However, it didn't take long for us to realize that this very special man would soon find a very special place in our hearts.

My husband and I went to the parish rectory on the afternoon of Monsignor's arrival to introduce ourselves, and to offer any assistance that he might need in getting settled. He came to the door wearing an old pair of khakis and a faded shirt, looking as if he had just gotten home from a round of golf or a day of fishing. When we walked into the living room, I'm sure my gasp was audible enough for him to hear.

Tackle boxes and fishing rods were leaning against the highly polished tables along the wall. Fishing lures were stuck in the shades of the crystal lamps that sat on the end tables. It appeared that Monsignor wanted his home to have that *lived-in* appearance, and it certainly did! He put on no airs and only wanted people to feel comfortable and at-home in his home.

Over the next four years, our parish family came to love this very down-to-earth man, who lived his faith by appreciating the simple things in life. He was often heard to say, "Every day is a good day because something good is going to happen. You just have to watch for it." And watch he did, whether it was playing a round of golf, sitting on a fishing bank, or meeting with a parishioner. He looked for the good in people and shared his love with others.

Many of us looked forward to the short three- or four-minute reflections that Monsignor gave at daily Mass. One morning his sermon touched us when he said, "We're so caught up in our hectic world that we don't take time to hear God."

He continued by saying we've lost our sense of God and who He is. Thus, we've lost our sense of sin. Everything seems okay in today's world. Monsignor told us we needed to "go to the mountain" and be with God to find out why we're here. He also had a deep love for Mary and talked about a lady who turned all of her cares over to Mary each day. What a beautiful way to approach life.

Another time he talked about being a hypocrite. He said we all probably have things that we hide deep inside, but that's okay. He cautioned, "Just don't let us become 'white glorious tombs hiding a pile of bones.'" With just a few simple words, Monsignor always left us with a message to take home—a message by which to live.

The children, too, loved this wonderful priest. My two daughters were three and four years old at the time of his arrival in Hugoton. I cleaned the rectory once a week and took the girls with me. I always reminded them that they must play quietly and not bother Monsignor, but invariably, within ten minutes of our arrival, Monsignor would have the girls in his office and I could hear him telling them fascinating stories about his life in Alaska.

This special Monsignor George Husmann would also show them pictures of the many places he'd been. He would tell them stories of the saints, and of course, St. George was one of his favorites. He was the one who told my girls to set their shoes out on December 6th so St. Nicholas would fill them with goodies. That became a tradition that my young daughters loved, and to this day, they (now ages twenty-three and twenty-four) look for a small gift on this feast day. My husband and I always laughed and said, "Thank you, Monsignor."

My daughters loved going to confession with Monsignor. They said it was just like "talking to Grandpa." Before they would leave the confessional, he always reminded them to "pray for old priests." I remember one day going into confession right after my seven-year-old daughter had come out. Monsignor was just sitting there laughing. I couldn't imagine what my child had told him, but he certainly was enjoying whatever it was.

He did tell me that she had said her last confession was six weeks ago and she said it was all her mother's fault! What a chuckle Monsignor got from that one. He loved the stories told by the children, and they loved hearing his. A loud cheer would always go up from the young children in the afternoon CCD classes when they saw Monsignor coming to visit.

He loved celebrating Halloween, too, and encouraged the children to come by his house for trick-or-treat candy. They loved dressing up in their costumes and going to see Monsignor. He would "ooh" and "ah" over their wild attire and tell them all about "All Hallows Eve" and what this holy day means to the Church. What a captive audience he had and what better way to teach the faith!

Once, in an interview, Monsignor said, "Most people never live. When they're young, they dream about how good it's going to be when they're old; and when they're old they regret what they did yesterday, and the day passes them by." Monsignor George Husmann taught us how to live and how to love.

Annette Sosa   *Hugoton, Kansas*

His Only Desire

One night, a young couple came to the rectory and asked to talk with me. They wanted to be married, but had a very big problem—the girl's father was totally against his daughter getting married. I offered to speak to him about it, but was advised not to approach him. Although he was Catholic, he was angry at the Church and would never be willing to meet with a priest. I was also told that he was keeping his daughter at home to use her for prostitution.

After some time had passed, the couple returned to see me. This time they came with the news that her father was now allowing her to get married. The first time I saw the bride's father was at the altar when he gave his daughter in marriage. I was unable to talk to him then, and did not see him after the ceremony.

Months later, as I was visiting a parishioner and other patients in the hospital, I came across this man and stopped in his room to say hello. It was the first time I had ever spoken to him. He was very surprised to see me and reacted by saying that he never asked for a priest, he was not sick at all, and that he was going home soon.

I went to the same hospital the following week, and the week after that. On both occasions, I found this man and approached him, and both times he had the same negative attitude. The fourth week I went again, but this time he was not there.

Soon after I returned home, the man's daughter came to see me and asked if I had been visiting her father in the hospital. Her father didn't know my name, but he remembered that I had been the celebrant at her wedding. The girl told me that her father had been transferred to another hospital, and that he was very sick. He wanted me to visit him.

When I arrived at the hospital that same afternoon, the nurse told me that the doctor wanted to talk to me. When we met, he asked me to try to persuade the man to eat something and take his medicine because he was refusing everything. He told me the man kept saying that the only thing he wanted was to see a priest so he could die in peace with God.

When I entered the dying man's room, he was in tears and was very apologetic for his previous attitude. He asked me to give him the last rites, and said he wanted to make peace with God. After we did this together, I suggested that he eat some food and take his medicine, but he wouldn't. He said his only desire was to have a happy death. His daughter was by his side when he passed away that evening, and before he died, he thanked her for bringing me to his bedside, and said he wanted me to perform the funeral service for him.

Fr. Edwin Agius, MSSP   *Parkville, Victoria, Australia*

Comfort in Difficult Times

Although I have met many good priests over the years that I could say good things about, there is one in particular who has helped me tremendously on my journey through life. His name is Padre Gerardo, and I met him many years ago when he was newly ordained and assigned to our parish.

When we first met this special priest, my husband and I were having many bad fights that made our children suffer. One day my husband decided to go to our church to talk about our problems with Padre Gerardo, and my husband made me look really bad. Usually the priests and other people my husband confided in believed him, and they would advise me to stop doing what my husband said I was doing wrong. Padre Gerardo, to my surprise, was different. He told my husband, "I heard what you have to say about your wife, but now I would like you to go and tell your wife to come to see me because I want to hear her side of the story." I couldn't believe it when my husband told me this!

When I went to see Padre Gerardo, I discovered that this priest had a beautiful soul and a great love for Our Lord and for Mary, our Blessed Mother. He has become my spiritual director and has helped my children and me more than anybody else could have.

One time, when my husband and I had a big problem, my oldest child, who was about twelve years old, went to church to get some help. Padre Gerardo gave him the comfort, guidance, and understanding that he desperately needed. On August 11, 2002, my beautiful twenty-eight-year-old son left us and Padre Gerardo celebrated a special Mass for him without my asking for it. I will always be very thankful for the understanding, the spiritual guidance, and the care he always showed to my precious child.

Padre Gerardo was transferred to a church in Fontana, California, and although he doesn't live near us anymore, he never forgets my family or me. One day, after I lost my child, I had been crying a lot and feeling desperate. I just wanted to die to go and be with my child. Crying, I left my house and went to my daughter's home. While I was there, I received a phone call. It was Padre Gerardo.

This thoughtful priest said he had been looking everywhere for me. He told me that he had called my home, my workplace, and my cell phone before he found me at my daughter's house. He said he had been kneeling in prayer when my name came to his mind, and that was why he had been looking for me. I know in my heart that Our Lord and the Blessed Mother knew I needed help, and they called Padre Gerardo to give me comfort in those very difficult times. God bless Padre Gerardo!

Alicia L. Marquez   *Indio, California*

Father Ron's Blessings

In April 1984 we welcomed into our home Autumn and Honey, two little girls who had suffered from abuse and neglect. At the tender ages of only two and one-half and three and one-half years, they came to us with three venereal diseases and physically, emotionally, and sexually abused and traumatized by their natural father.

We lived next door to St. Bartholomew Catholic Church in Newaygo, Michigan, and I will never forget Father Ron Schneider, the pastor at that time. He would have our *family* over, and he and his dog would get down on the floor and play with the little girls. He would read to them, trying to gain their trust. During the winter months, daily Mass was held in a special living room, and Father Ron let them become special altar servers. As both girls were very ill with cystic fibrosis, he received special permission for them to make their first Communion early.

Little did we know that Autumn Marie would leave us on March 11, 1987, at the young age of six and one-half years. But during her short life with us, Father Ron became her best friend, in line right after her newly adopted father. Father Ron would come to our house and spend time with the girls, and when Autumn died, he was there for Honey until her new sister, Pooja, arrived from Mother Teresa's orphanage in Bombay, India. We have always appreciated the extra time that he gave us to help us conquer the fears and win the trust and love of these special children of God.

John and Helen Botschka   *Newaygo, Michigan*

Walking With Us

I assisted Father Martin Hyatt in his work with teenagers in the Teen Encounter program at St. Basil's when he was in his mid thirties. That was when I first saw the gentleness and goodness of this young priest, and witnessed firsthand his dedication to his vocation. What I remember most about this remarkable priest, though, is the help and support he unselfishly gave me when my father was ill and dying of cancer.

I remember the night I got the news that cancer was causing my father so much pain in his back. My first reaction was to pray and ask God to help me help my dad in whatever way was needed. My second thought was to go to Father Martin with my need for help. When I approached him I said, "Please, help me make this time holy for my dad, and for all of us."

From that moment forward, Father Martin walked every step of the way with my dad, my children, and me. His prayers, his visits to the hospital, and his witness of God's love for us are indelible in my mind and soul. He visited Dad in the hospital, listened when I needed a caring ear, and supported my children in my absences.

Remarkably, I was with my dad that long last day when his soul was struggling so to separate and move on towards the heart of Jesus. I didn't call anyone, but as day turned to night, I was feeling tired and alone, and I was wondering how long Dad's suffering would continue. I prayed that I could stay the course to see him home.

Then in came Father Martin, who also brought along my cousin Claire, who I look up to as a model of Christian womanhood. We held Dad, sang quietly to him, and prayed for a gentle, peaceful, and holy passing. And so it was, on September 25, 1986.

Father Martin was at the funeral Mass, and on October 4, the Feast of St. Francis, he said a special Mass for Dad, with only my son Jonathan and me seated at the altar. His support has never wavered and continues in my life in countless ways, always loving as Jesus would, and always calling us to be what God wants.

Father Martin truly lives out his holy orders. I know him well and know that, even though he may feel differently, he always acts with love and acceptance. He lives his vows, and in all ways, he is the love of Jesus alive on the earth. As the institutional church struggles to find its center and renew its mission, it is priests like Father Martin who keep those of us who struggle, and sometimes lose our way, close to God—God who loves and saves us all. It is the *Father Martin-like* priests who guide us to the heart of Jesus.

Ann Mulrooney   *Jefferson, Massachusetts*

Stop! Someone Needs You!

At the age of twenty-six, I started walking away from my idea of who God is. In a paradoxical way, it was the beginning of my journey to a real understanding of who He really is. This wasn't a conscious, deliberate rejection of God in my life. I didn't say, "I don't want or need you anymore, God." I just got too busy with the business of living and making a life for myself, and over the years forgot to go to church, forgot to pray and forgot who I was.

After a while, I noticed that I was working harder, and that life kept getting tougher and more joyless. I found it harder to smile, harder to be kind, easier to be cross, and easier not to care. It was as though my heart had become smaller, harder, and colder, until I didn't feel like *me* anymore. The *me* I remember liked everyone and loved to laugh, sing, and play. The person I now saw in the mirror didn't like anyone very much—including herself. I knew something was wrong. I knew I was sick inside. I didn't know how sick, but God did.

At thirty-six years old, I was diagnosed with cancer and told I had a twenty-five percent chance of survival. I was scared, unhappy, and lost. The only thing I knew I could do was cry out to a God I hoped existed. That is exactly what I did, and He answered. He answered with power and might, and in quite a miraculous way. He reached down and swept me up into His arms in a way I could not miss or misunderstand.

I had been sent to the hospital for a bone scan, and as I waited for the test, I began walking the halls looking for a priest. After three floors, I realized I wasn't going to find one that way, so I went into the pastoral care center. There I was assured that a priest could be located because there were four Catholic churches in the area.

First, the lady in the pastoral care center called the front desk to inquire about the availability of a priest at the hospital. No priests were available, and none were expected that day. She then called the four Catholic churches in the area. The first one she called had no priest available. Then, to my dismay, neither did the second, third, or fourth church that she called.

Devastated, I went into the inner room of the pastoral care center to wait and pray until I was called for my test. As I prayed, I got angrier and angrier with God. "Why would you put me into a church that believes I need a priest to come fully back into your grace, and then when I am broken and need you, there are no priests? What kind of a God are you?" I demanded.

Just then, the phone rang, and I heard the lady at the desk say, "Oh yes! Send him right down." Minutes later, a very large priest walked into the room.

He listened to my story, heard my heartfelt confession and gave me absolution, and I received Communion for the first time in many years. God was in that room. Overwhelmed, and with tears in my eyes, I said, "Thank you. You don't know what a godsend you are." The priest replied with tears in his eyes, "No, you don't know what a godsend I am…" Confused, I looked up at him and he explained.

"I am a mission priest from up north and I've been working here in Florida doing a mission in Titusville. I only came to Melbourne to go to

101 Inspirational Stories of the Priesthood

the mall to shop. I began to feel badly and was on my way back to the parish when I heard, 'Stop. Someone needs you.' I looked up, saw the hospital, shook my head, and kept going. Then I heard it again, only louder and more insistent, 'Stop. Someone needs you.' So I stopped, went to the front desk and asked, 'Who is it that needs me?' They sent me to you."

God had pulled His priest right off the street to take care of me!

Six months later, I was telling my story to a church group when a lady stood up, interrupted me, and told the last half of my story. Surprised, I asked how she knew my story and she said, "He was our mission priest, and your encounter was the focus of our mission weekend—how God still uses His priests to heal His people, and His people to heal His priests!"

I want you to know that whatever church had ministered to me that day when I was so desperate is where I would have gone. Our heavenly Father took great pains to make sure that it was the Catholic Church that embraced me. I was lost and now I am found. I was sick and He made me whole, frightened and He gave me peace of heart, full of pain and sadness, and He gave me joy—so much joy! And it happened because of a nameless mission priest who was humble enough to answer the call to "stop" because someone needed him.

My dearest hope is that somehow this priest will read this book, and remember our encounter too. Thank you to this obedient and wonderful priest. I'm eternally grateful that you stopped.

Kathleen M. Ellertson   *Moore, Oklahoma*

I Thought I Knew My Faith

This story begins with a young people's weekend retreat back in 1962. I was a young woman who had been raised in the Baltimore Catechism days, and I really thought I knew my faith. Then, into my world, that

50

weekend came a young, attractive Jesuit priest who would turn my understanding of Catholicism upside down. His name was Father Armand Nigro.

The retreat is still fresh enough in my mind that I can quote portions of it from memory. This is because of Father Armand's wonderful clarity in teaching what the Gospels are all about.

He taught us that the word *church* should be thought of as a clan or family; that we belong to a *who* rather than to a *what*. Before this, my immature understanding of the church was somehow limited to the picture of the Vatican. Father Nigro's teaching of Jesus Christ also left a deep impression on me that weekend. He introduced me to a Jesus who cried, felt fatigue, and suffered a hideous death because He loved us enough to die rather than compromise the truth of how much we are loved.

Years later, I had the privilege of attending Father Armand's weekend lectures in Vancouver, British Columbia. At that time, he was also teaching full time at Gonzaga University in Spokane, Washington where he had a class of approximately one hundred men and women. Despite his full schedule, each weekend at the lectures he returned our papers, marked with his thoughtful comments. This type of schedule and dedication was his norm for over forty years.

A couple of years ago my husband and I met up with Father Armand again at a retreat we went to. As an older priest, his homilies have the richness and flavour of a rich red wine. One lasting effect of this retreat is that my good husband, who had enjoyed being a once-a-week Catholic, now makes sure that Scripture meditation is part of his daily routine.

Retirement from teaching hasn't dimmed Father Nigro's enthusiasm for spreading the Good News of salvation. He is now very happy to be completely available anytime people invite him to speak. This good priest has been a life-giver to me as well as to hundreds of others whose lives he has touched.

Joan A. Pogson   *Saanichton, British Columbia, Canada*

Questions of Doubt

The first time I questioned my faith was in 1962, when I was a young adult, and it shook me deeply. Because of my doubts, I didn't know if I should continue receiving holy Communion, or if I could even still be considered a Catholic. I went to confession and the Redemptorist priest listened kindly to me. Then he said, "I have never heard questions like these before, and can't answer them. I will do some research, and when you come in next week, tell me that you are the person for whom I looked up information."

Talking about my doubts that day helped me to minimize them, and I was even able to laugh at myself. The next week I felt foolish mentioning this to the priest, and thought he had probably forgotten about my questions. But then I said to myself, "Suppose he did look up the answers. It wouldn't be very nice if I didn't acknowledge the research he did for me."

I went back to the priest and said, "I'm the person who spoke to you last week about some doubts I was having about our faith. It helped me to talk it out, and I realize now that there are no answers to my questions." He was very happy, and reached his arm out around the curtain to hand me a piece of paper. He had written down the information that he had looked up for me. I still have that paper, and it is very precious to me. Since then I have lived comfortably with my questions. I don't know the priest's name but will never forget his wisdom and kindness.

Mary Maguire   *West Palm Beach, Florida*

Finding Jesus in a Hooch

I met Chaplain Traczyk in 1995–1996 when I was in the United States Marine Corps. Everyone in the Marines gets a nickname, and his was Chaplain Tragic because it rhymed with his last name. He was a Catholic priest assigned to the Second Battalion, Second Marines. Catholic chaplains are rare in the military, and he was only the second Catholic priest I met in the six years I served in the Marine Corps.

Our first meeting was on the island of Veaques near Puerto Rico. I can remember when our helicopter landed on the island. We got off and looked around the area; there was nothing but thorn bushes and horse manure everywhere. We had two whole weeks to live in this environment, practicing live fire.

Just after landing, however, we learned that we were in the wrong landing zone. We were supposed to be on the other end of the island, and so we began marching. It was blisteringly hot that day, and we were loaded down with our gear, weapons, ammo, and supplies. Needless to say, it was rough going. As we neared our objective, we faced a huge hill. We were all tired and drenched with sweat, and we dreaded going up. We approached the hill and met another company sprawled along the sides of the trail, resting and trying to cool off.

I looked at the hill and swore to myself. Then I was suddenly amazed: a solitary figure was coming down the hill. As he drew near I saw that it was a chaplain—Chaplain Tragic. He was loaded with as much gear as we were, and like us, he was suffering from the heat.

"Hey, chaplain!" I yelled. "Where's your R.P.?" meaning his religious programmer, an aide to the chaplain.

"I let him rest back at the command post but decided to come out and see how you guys are doing," he replied.

I then invited him to stick with us for the day, and he did. He turned right around and went back up the same hill he just came down! Talk about someone who will walk with a friend for two miles instead of only one. Then we parted, to meet again at a later time.

Our second encounter occurred on the island of Sardinia in the Mediterranean Sea. It had rained on that island for a week straight. We were all muddy, wet, tired, and basically angry at everything. On top of it all, I was coming down with bronchitis.

I was so angry with reality that I decided to get out of my hooch (my shelter) and scream. Yet I saw Chaplain Tragic standing outside in the rain. He was just as muddy as we grunts were, but still he seemed peaceful about it all. I yelled to him, "Hey, Chaplain! Tell your boss to cut this crap out!"

"Why don't you ask Him?" he asked with a smile.

"Show me where He is, and I will," I said.

So he led me to his hooch and pointed at a small cross outside the shelter.

"There He is now," he said. "Talk to Him."

I looked angrily at the cross and said, "Dear Lord, cut this crap out! Amen."

The chaplain then forcefully grabbed my military hat off my head and powerfully slammed it into my chest.

"You are talking to the Lord!" he said. "Show some respect! Take off your cover!"

Humbled, I knelt down and prayed: "Dear Lord, cut this crap out. Amen."

He then assured me that the Lord had indeed heard my cry, and I went back to my hooch.

The very next day the weather cleared. The sun was shining and the air was warm. I was sitting in a mud puddle with my cover over my eyes, meditating and enjoying the rays.

Suddenly, I heard some boots tromping and sloshing through the mud. A hand reached down, grabbed my cover, and lifted it. I saw it was the chaplain with a huge grin on his face as if to say, "See, I told you so."

I never forgot the priest and man who was *Chaplain Tragic* to his close friends. It's been some years now, and I'm out of the military. I am now in the seminary, fourth year of theology. I hope to meet him again to thank him for his examples of endurance (as the first event showed me) and faith (as the second event taught me). I hope to resume contact with him so I can invite him to my impending ordination.

John J. Forbus   *Houston, Texas*

What Can I Do For You?

I first met the eminent theologian and writer, Father John Hardon, SJ, when he moved into St. Joseph's Home in Detroit in the late 1990s. These were to be his last few years on earth, and his witness was inspiring to many, including me. His life was made-up of many day-to-day assents to God.

Father Hardon lived in the quarters above the chapel where he said Mass daily. Regardless of the hour, anytime he passed through the chapel and found a handful of people there, he'd say, "Let's celebrate Mass!" This kept the sacristan, Sister Mary Judith, hopping.

He loved the Mass so much that when the chaplain or any other priest said Mass in the chapel, you could always find Father Hardon in the back pew. He even went to the chaplain every day for confession because he wanted to be very pure when his turn came to celebrate the Mass.

Once, while in his room, he broke his fingers in the window. Though it was obvious they were broken, he went on to say Mass for all of us, and then went to the hospital.

When Father Hardon had eye surgery, he celebrated Mass that same evening with trembling hands and a patch over one eye. He frequently went about the halls of St. Joseph's Home blessing and thanking everyone:

employees, residents, the sisters, visitors, etc. He brought springtime to the home in the years he lived there. He brought Christ.

This holy priest never had a moment for himself. People came and called from all over the world seeking his counsel. He was always gracious to everyone, saying, "What can I do for you?" even when it was plain that he was exhausted with age and poor health.

He made sure that the sick and dying were not forgotten, and often said Mass in their rooms or homes, anointing them and giving the last sacraments. When he was on his own deathbed, he spent his last hours, up until his last breath, repeating this prayer: "I give you my heart, I give you my soul. I love you!"

Meeting Father John Hardon in his final years was a blessing to me. I didn't know him as the great writer and theologian as many others did. I just met a priest of God, grown old and humble, preaching by action the gifts of patience, strong faith, perseverance, hope, and so much love. He truly is "a priest forever in the line of Melchizedek."

Brigid M. King   *Macomb TWP, Michigan*

God's Control Tower

Father Daniel Mode, the pastor of my church in Alexandria, Virginia, is a living example of the results of persistent prayer. He told me the following story two years ago while I was visiting him at his office at Queen of Apostles Church.

At the time of Father Mode's birth, his mother was very worried because she had previously experienced many miscarriages. She did not want to go through the trauma of losing another child, so she began to pray fervently for the baby to survive. In fact, the baby did survive—or should I say babies—since she was carrying twins.

When the twins were born, Mrs. Mode prayed a very special prayer for her babies.

By the time Daniel was a teenager he already knew that he wanted to be an airline pilot. He was obsessed with flying, in fact. He built a complete cockpit in his room which he *flew* every day, and constructed a control tower in the hallway outside his room.

But one afternoon, during a meal at a family reunion, someone was passing him the mashed potatoes when he heard the words: "Dan, you are to become a priest."

"I heard this voice just as clear as I can hear you right now," Father Mode told me as I sat across from him. "I didn't actually hear it with my ears. It was inside, but I heard it so clearly that there was no mistaking it at all."

After hearing the voice, the boy sat back in his chair, still holding the plate of Aunt Jean's steaming mashed potatoes and staring into space.

"I asked myself if I had actually heard what I thought I had heard," he said. "I knew positively I had heard the voice because it was so clear, but being a priest was definitely not what I had in mind for my life. I already knew I was going to be a pilot."

Then, while he was still holding the mashed potatoes, he heard the exact same words a second time: "Dan, you are to become a priest."

"The second time I heard it I knew without a doubt that I was being asked to become a priest. It was clear that I hadn't imagined anything," said Father Mode.

The day Daniel Mode was ordained, his mother confided to him a secret she had never told him before: She had prayed her special prayer every day that he would be called to the priesthood.

Craig C. Turner

Burke, Virginia

The Apology

In a way, Msgr. O. F. O'Connor is the *grandfather* of my own vocation to the priesthood. When my family and I started going to the Cathedral of Our Lady of Lourdes in the early 1980s, an intriguing impression was always left on me by that mystical monsignor who punctually glided out of the sacristy in his riveting regalia just as the Lamb of God was intoned.

Monsignor would then humbly approach the tabernacle to procure the ciboria for Communion, ever clutching the sacred vessels with a palpably devout hunger for their content. Then he would stomp forward to take up his cherished post of sacred duty in feeding the flock with the body of Christ.

After Communion, Msgr. O'Connor would march back to return the ciboria to the tabernacle, and then, as if in perfect imitation of his Master, he would withdraw from the altar without a word. It seemed he would appear for almost every Mass, and also would invariably be hearing confessions when my time of the month came to receive the sacrament of reconciliation. I couldn't help but marvel at the single heartedness of such a priestly soul who apparently never had anything better to do than bring Christ sacramentally to the world. Indeed, what could be better?

After I entered Bishop White Seminary in 1986, the rector of the cathedral, Father Ribble, offered me a part-time job there, which, of course, was a welcome opportunity to get to better know both him and the mysterious Msgr. O'Connor. On days when Mass was not scheduled in our chapel, I was occasionally inspired to bike the few miles downtown for the 6:30 a.m. Mass that was faithfully celebrated by Msgr. O'Connor.

On one memorable day in Lent, threatening clouds tried to convince me to stay home. I dismissed the dark sky as the devil daring me to skip Mass, and resolutely set out for the cathedral anyway. I arrived dampened by nothing but a few drops of sweat. Right at the end of Mass, however, a distinctly audible downpour began, such that I was half-drenched just in the time it took to unlock my bike. Though I had been deaf to prudence earlier, I now welcomed her timely suggestion that I implore Msgr. O'Connor to give me a ride back to the seminary for my first class. However, after hearing my plea, to my surprise, he refused.

Although monsignor mumbled some very reasonable excuse, I can't remember it now since it was flushed out of my head as I struggled with my ten-speed bike to practically swim back to the seminary through a deluge existentially evocative of Noah's day. What I remember most, though, was what happened a few days later when I was thoroughly dried out again and turned up for my job at the cathedral.

There stood Msgr. O'Connor, restlessly waiting to apologize for not giving me a ride in the rain. I assured him that there was no need to apologize, since I had only myself to blame for imprudence in ignoring the weather warnings. I cheerfully added that the experience had turned into a memorable adventure, but he persisted in his humble apology. That example often haunts me when I am amiss and reluctant to even consider apologizing for not going the extra mile as enjoined by Christ.

In 1989, as I was preparing to depart for my studies in Europe, I collected advice from many mentors. I expected some gem from Msgr. O'Connor as I took my leave of him, and his gruff words still ring clearly in my head. "Pray, Rory, just pray. Nothing else matters." That's all he said.

Such simple counsel certainly didn't seem very sublime or practical at the time. And yet, months later when I was beset with crises and doubts and temptations to leave the seminary, his words, "Pray, just pray" was the redeeming refrain that reminded me of the one reliable remedy. And even today, no matter what hardship or confusion arises, my first course of action and favorite pearl of great price with advice to pass on to others is still best expressed with those wise words from Msgr. O'Connor: "Pray, just pray!"

Fr. Rory K. Pitstick   *Okanogan, Washington*

Discovering the Missing Piece

The year was 1996, and after spending eleven years in a very large parish and being one of the nameless multitudes, I longed to feel part of a community. While the church and liturgies were beautiful, there was something missing. Because of my shyness in groups, attempts to join in at even family events left me high and dry.

About the same time, my son began attending a Catholic school, St. Clement Mary Hofbauer in Baltimore. My family decided to *try out* the church, and would go to Mass there one weekend and then to our parish the next.

St. Clement is not a small church by any means. With about 1,800 families, it can be considered medium-sized. Nonetheless, it was significantly smaller and cozier, both in terms of building size and people size.

The Conventual Franciscan Friars reside at St. Clement. In those days, the friars would station themselves outside the three main exit doors of the church after Sunday Masses and greet people. The heart of Franciscan hospitality was very self-evident in this kindness.

It was our fourth or fifth time going to Mass there and my family was weighing whether we should join. My son delighted that he could see his teacher and some school friends at church, and my husband and I liked the homilies and the genuineness of the friars. But yet we weren't sure.

On one particular Sunday, Father Timothy Kulbicki, OFM Conv., was waiting at the side of the church. I would usually just bow my head, smile and move on, as the men in the family would shake hands with the priest. This Sunday was different. Father Tim extended his hand purposefully to me, smiled, and said, "It's nice to see you here again today." And he meant it!

After only four or five visits to the parish, not all in row, and not with the same presider, here was someone who remembered our family. Here was someone who didn't even know our names, but recognized us as being *part of the family.* He recognized us as being part of the body of Christ.

Thanks to Father Tim, my family discovered its missing piece. We found a home in the faith community of St. Clement.

Elizabeth Goral-Makowski   *Baltimore, Maryland*

NOTE FROM SISTER PATRICIA: Three stories came from Oregon; three letters all praising the works of Father Gary Zerr, the former pastor at Sacred Heart Parish in Tillamook, Oregon. As a friend of our community, he was telling us that he was not aware of the difference that he was making in the lives of his flock until he left the parish. Upon his departure, Father Gary received a box of letters—each one from a member of the church who had written him a special thank you for his wonderful sermons. While these three stories are a testimonial to one individual priest, this is surely not an isolated incident. No doubt there are thousands of priests who do not realize the impact their words have on those who hear them.

Personalizing the Message of Jesus

Ever since I can remember, I have wanted to experience spirituality. I tried many ways to be and feel spiritual. My expectations were somewhat extreme in the sense of what I felt should be the true feeling of spirituality. My expectation of what I perceived should be the true feeling of spirituality was an aura of a euphoric feeling of wholeness inside a contented heart.

Over the years, none of the expected perceptions came collectively. I always had the feeling of missing something, and my search for the spiritual relationship continued for years.

When Father Gary Zerr came to Sacred Heart Church in Tillamook, Oregon, his presence changed my life and fulfilled my journey for my search of spirituality.

Whenever Father Gary gives a homily, he has the gift and talent to personalize the message of Jesus. He can impact you with a sense of being with Jesus and the Disciples in the text of the message. His manner pulls you into the Gospel to focus on the lesson and message with total understanding. The command that has to reach each of us is very deep.

Father Gary was able to fill my feeling of emptiness, to experience true spirituality in my life today. I no longer have the quest to find and experience spirituality. Through Father Gary Zerr my life today is full. I am eternally grateful.

Lucy Scholerman   *Bay City, Oregon*

A Great Shepherd

I am a cradle Catholic who was raised in a rural community in Oregon. From the time I can remember, my family attended Church every Sunday morning. It was our weekly ritual, along with Saturday night reconciliation once a month.

Since I was the sixth child in our family, I watched as our numbers dwindled. It always seemed to happen as soon as my siblings received their driver's license. I received my driver's license about the time Vatican II rolled around.

With only one child remaining, and the Church being turned upside down, my father stopped attending Sunday Mass. It would seem that our entire family had left the Catholic faith.

I moved away from this small community, and as luck would have it, I met my future wife. The luckiest part of it all was that she was a cradle Catholic. We started attending Sunday Mass on a regular basis but stopped because we basically were not getting much out of it.

Then the greatest thing happened. At Christmas Midnight Mass in 2001, we heard Father Gary Zerr, a new priest at the Sacred Heart Parish of Tillamook, Oregon. He had a way of presenting a homily that explained any question you could ask about our faith. It was as if my eyes had been opened, and for once I could understand what my parents had tried to teach me. Once again, we began attending Mass on a regular basis.

Then my mother got ill, and I asked Father Gary to come to the home to anoint her. All the family was present and very touched by the way he helped us cope with the loss ahead. It was a hard time for my father when my mother died. Father Gary visited with him, talking and helping him.

Soon after my mother's passing, my father started attending Church on Saturdays. My father has now been diagnosed with cancer, but his faith is so strong now that he is able to deal with all the issues surrounding his health.

Father Gary has moved on to another parish, but he still finds time to inquire after my father and to visit when he is around. I feel we owe our renewed faith to Father Gary—he is a great shepherd.

Douglas R. Steinbach

Bay City, Oregon

Lost In My Own Problems

For many years my Catholic faith was something I honestly took for granted. I was raised Catholic and went to a boarding school run by Carmelites, but I really did not understand my faith. Nor did I want to at that point. Sometimes ignorance is bliss.

For a long time I was terrified of going to reconciliation because of a painful incident that happened when I was child. I carried that hurt with me, and it caused me to do things that created even more pain in my life. I was totally lost in my own problems, absorbed in fear and anxiety. Although I recognized the reason for my troubles, I didn't want to do anything about it.

Everything changed at a midnight Mass on December 25, 2001. Father Gary Zerr, our parish priest at Sacred Heart Parish in Tillamook, Oregon, was the celebrant. During his homily, I was struck when he said something like, "We celebrate the birth of Jesus today so that we can find our way through this life to heaven. The only reason any of us can enter that kingdom is because of the one whose birth we celebrate today. We are all sinners; we have all sinned, and the debt of our sins can keep us out of the kingdom. The good news is that Jesus came to pay that debt, which no one of us could have possibly paid. 'For God so loved the world that He gave His only Son.' When we meet the Lord our hands must be sinless, our hearts clean, and our desire must be for Him alone."

His words that night started me on a journey of being able to let go of my pain, of going to reconciliation, and of dealing with all the issues that stemmed from that incident so long ago. I admire and respect Father Gary as a priest and for how he admits that it is only in our weakness that we are strong. I feel he is a better priest for sharing that.

Since then, Father Gary has continued to be a great teacher. He stresses that Catholics can't afford not to be educated about the truth in our contemporary society. When my husband and I attended RCIA sessions we learned so much about our Catholic beliefs. It deepened our faith and that helps us face the challenges in the world, especially the scandals and such. So I learned after all that, "Ignorance is not bliss."

Jeanette F. Steinbach   *Bay City, Oregon*

A Miracle Baby

Early in October 2003, a mother was close to giving birth to her third child. Since her experience in having her two previous children was very difficult and she had severe depressions, she was admitted to the hospital one month before this third baby's due date.

As before, the mother was severely depressed and therefore was given very strong anti-depressant medication every day until the time came for her to give birth. During this time, I visited the mother, giving her holy Communion and blessings often, and praying with her.

On the first day of November, the baby girl was born. But straight-away, it was known that the baby's brain was dead, and she was motion-less. She was transferred to another hospital where she was placed on a machine to see if she would respond. The parents were told that in all cases such as this the baby never survives. At this, many people in the parish, other friends, and I began praying during Mass, and we began asking for the intercession of our Blessed Mother.

Four days later, the parents called to tell me the doctors had advised them that there was no more hope and that they were going to turn the machine off. They asked me to baptize the baby in the hospital before all this happened.

It was Wednesday, the day our parish normally has the novena of Our Lady of Perpetual Help. We prayed during the Mass, and then I went to the hospital. During the thirty-minute drive I switched the radio off. I felt that this was going to be an extraordinary moment, so I prayed continu-ously while I was driving.

As soon as I arrived and met the family, I was told that the baby girl was moving her tiny feet very slowly. There was commotion in the ward and I thought it might not be an appropriate time to do the sacrament of baptism. When everyone calmed down, we all participated in the prayers, during which there was more excitement—the baby opened her eyes! After we finished the baptism, there were more signs of life in her hands; they were moving like a baby waking up from sleep.

When the doctor in charge visited and examined the baby, all he had to say to the parents was that, although he was not a Christian, this truly was a "miracle baby." Her brain was working as normal and she was recovering, something he had never before seen in his profession.

After three weeks, baby Brittonya was taken home. The case was reported on two television stations during current affairs programs, and a report also appeared in *Woman's Day* magazine. She is now a normal child, looking very healthy and walking around.

Fr. Edwin Agius, MSSP   *Parkville, Victoria, Australia*

My Three Miracles

I came home from the hospital in October 1987 unable to walk without the help of a walker. Although my foot had been saved after contracting a serious bone infection from five previous surgeries, all of my bodily functions were severely compromised, and I was required to take intravenous antibiotics which I had to administer myself. I was extremely weak and didn't know what my future was.

I had not been a very faithful Catholic for about twelve years. I knew I needed—and wanted—to be spiritually healed. I called the parish that we belonged to but was told the priest didn't make house calls. I called another parish, St. Thomas Aquinas, and talked with the pastor, Monsignor John T. Gulczynski. He said he would be over to my home right away.

Monsignor John sat with me at my kitchen table for three hours hearing my confession, giving me holy Communion, and anointing me. As he was leaving, he hugged me, gave me his blessing again and said he would pray for me. I promised him that as soon as I could walk, I would come to Mass.

My husband came home from work that night and surprised me with a brand new sterling silver rosary. We had only been in bed for a little bit when I needed to use the rest room. Without even thinking, I got out of bed and walked by myself without my walker into the bathroom. I never had to use the walker again.

The following day, while I was praying with my new rosary for the forty-five minutes it took to administer the antibiotics, my hands and forehead started to really burn where Monsignor John had anointed me. I didn't know what was happening but just kept on praying. When the intravenous antibiotic administration had finished, I put everything away. As I lay my rosary down, I noticed all the links had turned gold.

Within a few minutes, my sister called me from Illinois to tell me that Our Blessed Mother had appeared in Medjugorje and that rosaries were turning gold all over the world, as a call to conversion.

So I had experienced three miracles in less than twenty-four hours: a very holy priest had answered my call for spiritual help, I had received physical healing allowing me to walk by myself, and my new rosary had turned to gold.

One week later, on the feast day of Saints Simon and Jude, I drove myself to St. Thomas Aquinas for Mass which Monsignor John celebrated. Afterwards, I went to the rectory to become a parishioner. If it weren't for Monsignor John, I don't believe I would be where I am today in my journey to be what Our Lord wants me to be. I have a long ways to go, but thanks to Monsignor John, I'm on the right path.

On July 1, 2004, Our Lord called Monsignor John home at the age of ninety-two. He founded St. Thomas Aquinas Parish, in Dallas, Texas, on September 18, 1952, and is dearly missed.

Eternal rest grant unto him, oh Lord, and may your perpetual light shine upon him. May he rest in peace. Amen. Thank you, Monsignor John, from the bottom of my heart.

Kathy M. Metevier   *Dallas, Texas*

The Priest from China

I was collecting altar cloths and vestments to take home for cleaning when I had my first personal chat with Father Joe. He had just finished an Italian Mass and had come downstairs to change. Since he was Chinese, people thought it was funny that he said Mass in Italian and English. Father Joe is able to speak seven languages.

Several months later, I went to the rectory to ask for a priest to assist an elderly couple. The lady, Mrs. Reel, was in her 80s and had called for a priest several times, but none had gone to her home to visit. The first priest I approached was far too busy, and the second one walked away with no time to listen. I'd had it with this indifference and had raised my voice to the receptionist when Father Joe came into the office and asked if he could be of assistance.

After I gave him information about the couple, he promised he would visit them. Not only did Father Joe visit regularly, but he also took Mrs. Reel clothing shopping for her grandson who was confined to a hospital for mental illness. The boy's mother had died at thirty-five years old, and his father wasn't able to help him through the grief. All he had were his grandparents.

Every few weeks Father Joe took Mrs. Reel to visit her grandson and to do errands. He was very happy when our community joined in to support them with grocery shopping and cooking when needed. Also, the men and their sons helped with raking and bagging leaves for Mr. Reel who suffered from left-sided paralyses due to a stroke.

I loved playing the guitar and leading our adult folk group in song. We sang for our *Ultreya* Mass every month, which Father Joe agreed to celebrate for us (an *Ultreya* is a gathering of *Cursillo* friendship groups). He was so impressed with the faith of the people in the *Ultreya* group that he decided to go on a *Cursillo* weekend retreat himself. During his retreat, he blessed us with his sharing and openness.

Before his *Cursillo*, Father Joe didn't share his personal life with others. He was very reserved, and it went against his culture. Now he laughed, joked, played, and fully became one of the congregation in heart, soul and spirit. He was not just a priest, but a wonderful man who could be very humble and alive with joy.

Father Joe's humility and sense of humor gave many teenagers the freedom to be themselves at monthly Christian Awakening meetings held at our house. Young people love him. He was never afraid to tell them stories of his younger years and the problems he had.

When Father Joe went back to China we were all lost. We missed him so much. He came back to the United States to visit time and time again and would celebrate Mass in our home for us. He would also hear our daughter's confession, for he was her only confessor; she wouldn't go to anyone else.

This summer Father Joe came from Taiwan to visit us in Pennsylvania where we have retired. He stayed with us for six days and was in constant awe of the deer, chipmunks, and other wildlife we have in our backyard. Each morning before breakfast, Father Joe went for a walk in the woods for a few hours of prayer and meditation. Later in the day he would sit outside and watch the animals, trying to feed them. The birds and chipmunks would be right at his feet, and the deer would stand a few feet back watching him. Father Joe was so happy and at peace during those moments. He felt very blessed to be so close to God's critters.

Before he left, Father Joe celebrated another Mass in our home with our friends. We also had dinner with our parish priest, and a meal and confession at our daughter's home. This kind and holy man touched so many people with his humility and simplicity, with his caring and gentle soul, and God's love. There is no other way to describe him.

When Father Joe went back to Taiwan, saying goodbye was harder than usual. This time the trip was very physically challenging for him, and we knew he might not be able to visit us again. We will keep in touch by phone, letters, and e-mail.

Connie Andretta   *Milford, Pennsylvania*

We Have Seen Jesus

In 1967 I was seventeen years old and engaged to be married to a Catholic named Jon Davis. Several years prior to that I had experienced the Lord in a personal way, but did not attend church regularly. After meeting Jon I didn't think twice about becoming Catholic. We wanted to marry in the Catholic Church and raise our children with the Church as an important part of our family life.

At that time in our small town of Rushville, Illinois, Father Robert Reynolds was the priest at St. Rose Parish. He had recently brought this tiny mission church to parish status and had supplemented the parish income by teaching English and Latin in the local high school where I was a student. After class one day I asked him how I could "get to be a Catholic." That started a relationship that continued for the next thirty-five years and has been a total blessing for my family and for me personally as well.

Father Reynolds took me under his wing that day in 1967. He brought me to the Catholic faith, worked with Jon and me through our preparations to marry, and performed our wedding ceremony. Then one year later, he baptized our baby girl. Soon the Lord called him on adventures in other parishes and at a Catholic worker house.

Although our tiny church was hard-pressed to have a pastor of our own, the Lord provided and we continued to grow as a parish family. Many years passed, and then one Sunday we got word that Father Reynolds was coming back to us; he was *retiring* to our little parish. It seemed that he'd left part of his heart with us when he moved on to continue his ministry, and now he wished to return to us. He wanted to be our pastor and live out his senior years with us.

We settled into the wonderful life of a parish blessed by a teacher and mentor who was truly a good shepherd leading us along the path of Our

Lord. People young and old alike responded to Father Reynolds' wit and energy. His homilies, rather like a delicious thick gumbo, even moved me to take notes many days.

Eight more years slipped by, and one morning, two years ago, our devoted pastor had a stroke. Our parish was stunned, and we immediately began to pray for him. In my heart, I wondered what would become of our parish, thinking that surely Father Reynolds would have his hands full in the recovery process and would not be able to return as our priest. I was wrong!

Father Reynolds worked hard in his therapy, and before long was back at St. Rose for the Sunday morning Mass. In the time since his stroke he has voiced concern that he may be short-changing Jesus and the parish because he struggles at times during Mass and cannot do things one hundred percent. That has hardly been the case; we have not been short-changed at all.

In the time since Father Reynolds' stroke, we have seen Jesus shining brighter than ever through him. Our parish family is learning more from our good teacher than ever before. It is not only the Gospel teachings that we receive—we have been learning first-hand about perseverance and determination as we watch our friend and pastor persistently show up for Mass, continuing his ministry. We are also learning that it's okay to allow people to help you when you need it, and that one's usefulness is not over just because life has changed.

In a book by Henri Nouwen called *Can You Drink the Cup*, I read about the cup of life holding it all: the beautiful gifts and the sorrowful mysteries. We cannot separate things out and cast away that which is painful or does not suit us. Through Father Reynolds, I have seen God bring good out of a situation that was potentially devastating. He is drinking from the cup of life at the table of the Lord. I am glad to be at that table with him.

I have learned many things from this beloved friend and priest over the years. Perhaps the most valuable things have been what he has been teaching since he had his stroke, which was one of the greatest sorrows of his life. For the rest of my life I will recall what I have observed from him in the many years I have known him. I believe his choice to continue on in the best way he can, through God's grace, will inspire me and all those who know and love him. His example will give us the tools we need to do the same in our lives.

As Father Reynolds continues to preach the word of God to St. Rose Parish, the Good News comes to us in more ways than one as we read between the lines and watch as our humble pastor continues to do what he so deeply loves: being a priest and a member of the St. Rose family. St. Francis encouraged us to "preach the Gospel, and if we have to, use words." Father Reynolds is preaching the word to those who know him through actions that speak louder than words.

Mary Jane Davis   *Frederick, Illinois*

Hearts Beating As One

It was a cold, foggy night in 1997 as I trudged up the steps of St. Clement Mary Hofbauer Parish in Baltimore, Maryland to go to one night of a preached mission. In my mind, a mission involved setting up churches to spread the faith in places where there aren't many churches. So, what in the world was a *preached mission?* Curious to find out, I went.

The still filling, dimly lit church smelled faintly of beeswax. As I settled into the pew, I glanced towards the sanctuary and saw a very young man dressed in vestments seated in the presidential chair. I remember thinking two things. The first was that he looked exactly like the picture of St. Dominic Savio that Sister Mary Pieta showed us in fifth grade. The second thing I thought was that he had to be at least twenty-something, because there were rules about that sort of thing. I settled into the pew, wary about what this *youngster* might say. His name is Father Daniel Francis, C.SS.R.

The lights came up, the music began, and the Mass started. So far, so good. When it came time for the homily, I crossed my arms, leaned back into the pew, and tightened my jaw. I had predetermined that this young man would be an adequate preacher at best.

As Father Daniel moved from the ambo to the front of the altar to preach, I could feel my jaw unclenching, my arms dropping, my back straightening. You could feel the energy and attentiveness in the entire church. You could see the spirit of the Lord shining in and through this priest. When he began to speak, his love and zeal for God and souls burst through him like flames. What a beautiful transformation!

I have heard many good sermons in my time. I have seen priests preach with passion and grace. I have been blessed by their words and witness. Yet this was the first time I had ever seen someone so on fire for God.

That evening, Father Daniel spoke of God's desire for us. He relayed a story of when he visited his sister who was pregnant. He was so happy, because in his missionary work, he had never been around his sisters or sisters-in-law when they were full of child. While he baptized the babies, he did not get to do things like feel the baby kick against his or her mother's belly. He said he went with his sister to the obstetrician and was so excited he thought he could hear his heart beating: loud, strong, and fast. But, he said, it was the baby's heartbeat he was hearing through the monitor.

As tears streamed silently down my cheeks, he went on to say that God longs for us as if we were, we are, His heartbeat. At that moment, that young priest, so filled with fire, touched my soul with a flame of God's abounding love. At that moment, the Word became flesh in my soul once again. At that moment all I could do was cling gratefully to God who loves me, who loves all of us, with the greatness of His heart.

God speaks His word in the ordinary actions of our lives. By relaying a very ordinary, human experience, this priest touched my faith and helped my soul give birth to a new understanding of the Lord. God's goodness flowed through the instrumentality of Father Daniel. This humble beacon of God's grace broke through to lift the fog and darkness. How grateful I am!

Elizabeth Goral-Makowski   *Baltimore, Maryland*

I Am Finally Free

Back in the early part of 1987, while I was an associate pastor at St. Francis of Assisi Parish in Spokane, Washington, I went to visit an elderly parishioner at a local hospital. William Meulner had been in the cancer ward at Holy Family Hospital for a few weeks, and his condition was rapidly deteriorating.

I had been in the room for only a few minutes when the nurse walked in and asked for some time alone with William. So, I stepped back and she pulled the curtain closed. As I was waiting for the nurse to finish, I struck up a conversation with William's twenty-nine-year-old roommate, Mark Sonnenberg. He began to tell me a little bit about his life.

It turned out that Mark had been baptized and raised in St. Francis Parish, and had even attended the parish school. When he entered high school, his family moved across town into another parish. He said that as he got older, he drifted away from the faith and eventually quit going to church altogether. After we talked for about ten minutes, the nurse finished what she was doing and I turned my attention back to William. But before I did that, I promised Mark I would visit him again.

A week later, I returned to the hospital and found Mark in his own private room. With the added privacy, we were able to talk more freely. In the midst of our visit, I asked Mark if he would like to go to confession. He said it had been a long time since he had gone, and that he had lived a very sinful life. I assured him that God would forgive any sins he had committed, no matter how bad they were. With a little reluctance, he finally said, "Yes."

Right then and there, he poured out his heart to God, and tears began to flow. It was as if a floodgate had been opened and there was no way to close it. After giving absolution, I anointed Mark and he received Communion for the first time in years. Then the most beautiful smile came across his face as he said, "I am finally free."

One night, about three months after our initial meeting, I received a phone call from Mark's girlfriend. She asked me to please come to the hospital because Mark was not expected to make it through the night. I immediately grabbed my Bible and oil and went to be with them.

When I arrived, Mark's girlfriend was lying on the bed with him. Her arm was draped around his shoulders. She told him that I was there, and that everything would be all right. I administered the Last Rites and then sat down on a chair next to his bed and held his hand. About an hour later, Mark started gasping for air and took his last breath. It was the first time I had been with someone when he died.

To say his death had an impact on me is an understatement. As a priest, I had shared in Mark's life in ways that few others ever had. I saw him change from a young man afraid of dying to a man who had made his peace with God. What a blessing it was to have witnessed the power of God change a human heart. As the scriptures say, "There is more rejoicing in heaven over one repentant sinner than over ninety-nine righteous people who have no need of repentance." (Luke 15:7)

I am forever grateful for having known Mark, and for being a part of his life and death—and those of many others after him. But I am mostly thankful to God for allowing me to serve Him as a priest, even with all my weaknesses and faults. He never ceases to amaze me. And, as I think back to Mark's departure from this world into the next, I can almost swear that he had a smile on his face.

Fr. Michael G. Blackburn, OFM   *Spokane, Washington*

Secret Mass in the School

My family was living in Jeddah, Saudi Arabia, in 1984, as my father had a job there for Saudi Airlines. We are Filipinos and Catholics, but since we had no opportunity to celebrate the Eucharist, our family prayed the rosary together.

One day my father obtained information that a Catholic priest was celebrating Mass at a school in our vicinity every Friday to coincide with the week's end. What made these Eucharistic celebrations special was not so much that they were held clandestinely, but because there was a priest who was willing to lose it all to celebrate the Eucharist for us foreigners.

Even with the threat of deportation looming over our heads my parents took the whole family to the Masses at the school where I received my first holy Communion. I remember that day when my mother dressed me in a ruffled white blouse with white pants and explained to me that I was about to receive Jesus in holy Communion.

At the time, I could not fathom the gift of such a special encounter in Jeddah, Saudi Arabia, but I do remember feeling all warm and happy without really knowing why. I knew it was a special moment.

Two Fridays later, our car was prevented from proceeding to the school where the Mass was held because police patrolled the entire area. My father was advised by people who had already been sent back that our family should turn around and not attempt to reach the school.

News came out that there would be no more Masses because the brave priest had been deported. We never returned to the school and did not partake in Mass again until we returned to the Philippines.

I never knew that priest's name, but I would like to thank him for risking everything to celebrate the Eucharist for us.

Josephine R. Mata   *Quezon City, Philippines*

Compassion Overcomes Shame

I was born in 1947 to a devoutly Roman Catholic mother and a non-practicing Protestant, want-to-be Jewish father. My mother taught me to love God and the Church by participating fully and lovingly in her faith and seeing to it that my younger brother and I did the same. By the time I was in high school, I was helping the Holy Family Sisters teach Confraternity of Christian Doctrine (CCD) classes to public school children after school. I even believed for a couple of years in my early teens that I had a vocation to the religious life.

In April 1965 I was seventeen and ready to graduate from high school when I began my slow descent from good Catholic girl to turning away from God and the Church. For over thirty-five years I led a life of promiscuity, alcohol, and abortion. I experienced three failed marriages, a near-fatal car accident that left me partially disabled for life, two prison terms, a violation, a twenty-year heroin habit, and lots more.

But God evidently got tired of waiting for me to take the first step. He knew I was looking for Him and sent me two wonderful priests who helped me turn my life around, completely and permanently.

The year 2000 found me doing something I had not done in my thirty-five misspent years: I started praying again. I had forgotten most of the prayers I had learned as a child, but I bought some prayer books and started all over again. I started praying every day. I prayed constantly. I remember feeling as if I had to do something. At that particular time, there was a good chance my husband and I were going to get arrested again and do another lengthy prison term. We were just too old to start all over again, and I had an elderly dad I was trying to look after, too.

One morning, I found an early-morning Sunday Mass on a local television station led by Father Miles O'Brien Riley of San Francisco, and I began watching faithfully each Sunday morning at 5:30 a.m. After about a year, I wrote Father Miles and asked if I could possibly come to San Francisco and meet with him and tell him my story. He actually phoned me a week later and made an appointment for me to drive to San Francisco and see him.

I kept the appointment, and it was a life-changing experience. I just cried and told him about my entire life, all my sins, and all that had happened to me since I was seventeen years old. He was extremely understanding, did not judge me in any way, heard my confession, and gave me absolution and some advice about what to do next. He said even though I would have to have my previous marriages annulled, my current husband of ten years and I would have to be remarried in the church. He explained everything to me that I needed to know. And the best part of it all was he told me I could begin receiving the Eucharist again after thirty-five years. I was ecstatic.

After I returned home from this meeting, I was still hesitant about going to Mass at my local parish. I would need to meet with the pastor to talk about my past, possible annulments, and my desire to become a member of the parish. After a few weeks of just watching and participating in the televised Sunday Mass with Father Miles, I got up enough courage to go to Mass *in person*. I went, received communion, and it was the best thing that had happened to me since I was seventeen years old, and I was then fifty-two.

After about a month of going to Mass and receiving Communion, I phoned the parish business office and asked to make an appointment with the pastor, Father John Boll of Holy Rosary Parish in Woodland, California.

Father John was the answer to all my prayers. I knew from the moment I met him that I had nothing to fear. He made me feel as though I belonged in the Church, back with our Lord, forgiven and ready to begin my spiritual journey anew. He helped my husband and me deal with all the records and paperwork for our assorted annulments, and after a year, our previous invalid marriages were annulled, and we were married in the Church one Monday morning during Mass. It was the happiest day in my life. I was back in the Church, I was worshipping God once more, and joy filled my life. After talking at length to Father John, my husband decided he wished to become a Catholic, and with Father John's help and instruction, my husband is now a practicing Catholic.

Without first Father Miles and his TV Mass and willingness to reach out to me, and without the deep concern, compassion, acceptance and understanding Father John gave my husband and me, I would never have come back to the Church, as I would have been too ashamed and too afraid to try on my own.

I cannot ever express the love and gratitude I have for these two exceptional priests and what they did, not only in honoring their vows and the priesthood, but what they did for a lost, lonely, and floundering soul looking desperately to find her faith and religion after so many years without God in her life.

Father John and Father Miles, may God always bless and bestow his grace on you. Thank you for saving my life.

Josephine M. Shryock   *Woodland, California*

God's Instrument

I am a cradle Catholic. After my first marriage ended in divorce, I felt like I wasn't needed at our Catholic church anymore. I couldn't take part in any of the sacraments, so I stopped going to mass on a regular basis.

I remarried, and my new husband, Roger, was also a cradle Catholic. However, he had stopped going to mass during his teenage years because he felt as if he couldn't give enough alms at church. He came from a very poor family.

When it was time for my son to make his first Communion, we knew how important it was for us to be supportive of him, so we started going to mass again, but we still felt left out of the Church during Communion time.

Roger was stationed in the United States Army in Mainz, Germany, in 1984, and there we met an Army chaplain, Father Paul Bomba. Roger and I explained to Father Bomba that we felt left out of the Church. He told us we could get an annulment and rejoin the Catholic Church. He gave us all the pamphlets and reading material on annulments so we could get a better understanding of what we were in for.

While Father Bomba was getting to know us, he found out that I had a sewing machine and that I knew how to sew. It didn't take me long to start sewing all the baptismal garments for the babies who needed to be baptized. Being in the military, sometimes there were as many as fifteen baptisms a month. I finally felt like I was needed by the Catholic Church for the first time in years.

One day, before mass, Father Bomba asked Roger if he could help out with passing the basket for alms. Well, it didn't take long before Roger was in charge of collecting the money and counting it every Sunday morning. So Roger was also feeling like he was needed by the church.

Little did we all know that God was using Father Bomba to bring Roger and me back into the Church, where we felt needed, wanted and loved by God.

After Roger retired from the Army in 1986, we came back to the United States. I finally got my annulment from my first marriage. In 1989, Roger and I had our marriage blessed in St. Joseph's Catholic Church in Rayne, Louisiana, by Father Michael Russo.

We never saw Father Paul Bomba again, but, in 2004, we were finally able to get in touch with him through the Internet. I was able to tell him what he meant to Roger and me and what he did for our family by allowing God to use him as His instrument to bring us back to our faith through his kindness and patience. We will never lose contact with or forget Father Paul Bomba.

Debra R. Fusilier   *Rayne, Louisiana*

My Palm Branch Cross

I was a young teenager on Palm Sunday at St. James Parish in Seaford, New York, and the overflow crowds necessitated a separate Mass in the basement cafeteria of the school. It was standing room only, and I was just as glad, because my position in the back, close to the double doors, meant I would be one of the first to leave after Mass. I would wait outside on this beautiful day, feeling my independence, while my mother greeted neighbors and friends.

Leaning against the yellow cinder block wall with the green palm branches in my hand, I began folding the palm, this way and that, eventually forming a cross with it.

Father Codogan, an elderly missionary priest who had returned from Africa due to a tropical illness he acquired there after many years of service, was present at the Mass. Unbeknownst to me, he had been quietly watching me fold the palm branches.

During the announcements, Father leaned towards me, and in a quiet voice that seemed accustomed to whispering, asked, "Can I have that beautiful palm cross you made? I do not know how to make one like that. I will give you my palm branches in exchange."

I was surprised by his request, but of course I smiled and agreed.

I remember him to this day because he was the first priest to make me feel that I had anything of value to offer to the Church, and, however small, it was important. This event happened over forty years ago, and to this day, I contribute whatever bit of time and talent that I can to my parish because one priest recognized a small gift that I had as a teenager.

Patricia E. Wolf, SFO   *Hummelstown, Pennsylvania*

God Sent a Messenger

This story takes place in the summer of 2002, in Columbia City, Indiana. My girlfriend had suffered a bad accident and was fighting to hold onto her life. I was a complete nervous wreck, and every sort of bad thought was floating through my mind. It was then that I came into contact with Father Michael Lonigan.

I had never met Father Lonigan before this night, as I was new to the area and didn't know anyone except my girlfriend. This priest saw how stressed I looked and knew how touch-and-go my girlfriend's health was. He began talking to me, and the first thing he told me was a joke. Maybe it wasn't the best joke in the world, but it made me laugh and relieved some of the nervous tension I was feeling. Until then, I never knew a priest could have a sense of humor.

My girlfriend needed to endure a procedure that night to stabilize her condition, and Father Lonigan sat with me the whole night, praying with me and offering words of encouragement. This caring priest didn't know me at all, and yet the only thing he wanted to do was make me feel better. It came at a time when my faith was being tested fully; at a time when I didn't know why God was presenting me with such a challenge. God sent a messenger, Father Lonigan, to support me, comfort me, and to pray with me.

I have come to know Father Lonigan extremely well since that summer, and consider him to be not only a priest and mentor, but a grandparent figure in my life as well. This is due to his warmth, humor, and loving nature towards all people.

My girlfriend survived her procedure that night despite what many doctors considered difficult odds, and we are still together today. I firmly believe that it was the prayers Father Lonigan and I said together that allowed for such a healing to take place. I have never met a more wonderful man and priest than Father Michael Lonigan, and my girlfriend and I are honored that he will be presiding at our wedding one day.

Clint R. Novak   *Mt. Pleasant, Michigan*

Not a Saint, Yet!

"Be holy in all you do, since it is the Holy One who has called you, and Scripture says, 'Be holy, for I am holy.'" (1 Peter 1: 15)

Twenty years ago, if anyone had told me to be holy in everything I did, I would have laughed in his face. For years, I had turned away from God and had gone as far as leaving His church. Later, through several circumstances, I was jolted out of my complacency and literally dragged back to Mass, which I initially attended more out of duty than for love of God.

I remember standing outside St. James Catholic Church one sunny Sunday morning in Kinross, Tayside, Scotland. My mother had come to visit from Gibraltar and wanted to speak to our priest, Monsignor Benjamin Donachie M.A. Dip.Ed. He reminded her very much of her late brother in his appearance and in his musical ability, and she developed quite an affinity towards him. My uncle had been a Spanish composer who played the piano as Monsignor did, and both men were small in stature and full of personality and charisma.

As my mother conversed with Monsignor, he half-turned towards me with a smile on his face. It was obvious that he was referring to me when I overheard him say, "She is not a saint yet, but I am praying for her." This remark had a tremendous effect on me. Not only did it demonstrate his total trust in God, but also his certainty that his prayers for me would be answered. It made me realize, too, how important it was for me to change the way I was living my life.

Years later, God used Monsignor once again to bring me closer to Him, and this time it was during a holy hour. At the time, my mother-in-law was dying of cancer and had only one week to live. I remember kneeling in front of the Blessed Sacrament feeling totally distressed at the thought that she would die not knowing there was a God who loved her. Monsignor Donachie was leading the holy hour and I heard him say, "Yes, my child, tell me what is wrong. I am your heavenly Father who loves you. Give me your worries and I will help you." These words that flowed out of his mouth pierced my heart; I felt they were coming directly from God. This time I repented in earnest and gave God my life in return for the life of my mother-in-law.

Mum lived a full year after that holy hour, and died in a state of grace at St. Columba's Hospice in Edinburgh where she recited the Lord's Prayer with the nuns every day. Shortly after her death, three members of her family were converted and joined the Catholic Church. Monsignor Donachie was a tremendous support during this time and became a much loved and cherished friend in Christ. At that point my own life took on a new meaning. I was totally transformed and given a new life in Christ. Monsignor became my spiritual director and led me back to God through his example of faith, wisdom, and commitment.

I strongly believe in the power of intercessory prayer, and, in particular, the prayers of a holy man. Monsignor Donachie is indeed a holy and faithful man who has dedicated his entire life to our great God. He has remained committed to the Gospel and no doubt has helped many others besides me in their spiritual journeys.

Many years ago, God revealed himself to me through Monsignor Donachie, and I dearly thank Him for that. I also thank Monsignor for being a devout servant of God and for allowing the love of Christ to shine through him. His devoutness and the love of God changed my life. Praise God!

Maria V. Bartlett   *Kinross, Tayside, Scotland*

Finding My Vocation in Beirut

I used to be afraid of what people would think of me if they knew that the Lord speaks to me. Most people, I think, would assume I am crazy or on drugs. Perhaps there would be a few who would believe me and think me a saint or holy person. But I always believed that if I were to tell anyone that God talks to me, everyone would think me a freak, quite outside the normal range of people.

But God does speak to me, and I am no longer afraid or embarrassed to say so.

I do hear God speak to me, just like Moses did, and just like the apostles did in the gospel. The facts speak for themselves.

I have also come to realize that it doesn't mean people have to be holy, or even good, for God to speak to them. Consider Moses, to whom God spoke from a burning bush: Moses was running away from the authorities because he murdered an Egyptian fellow. Moses was no saint, yet God spoke to him. And what about St. Paul, a strong persecutor of the early Christians, who was spoken to by God on the road to Damascus? God spoke to an enemy of the early Church! And just like Samuel, just like the disciples, Andrew and Peter, when God spoke, all they could do was listen, follow, and obey. It is not that they were good or holy, but that God needed them, and, in hearing his voice and obeying it, they were to become holy. God's call is not just to the holy. God's call shows us the way to become holy. That is why he talks to people like me.

Finally, most important is what we learn from the gospels. God has chosen each of us, before we could ever choose God. And God is calling out to each and every one of us. Just because God speaks to an individual does not make that person unique or different from anyone else, because God is trying to speak to everyone. But not everyone hears, wants to hear, or, when hearing, believes what God is saying. God calls us because He has chosen whom He needs and wants in order to accomplish His plan. And God needs us!

My story begins in Beirut, Lebanon, in June 1982. A military invasion was underway. There were jets fighting overhead, bombs falling, shrapnel raining down, the sound of machine gun fire and bombs exploding, and thousands dead. I was in hiding and trying to get to safety over the mountain road to Damascus. But I was trapped, and then captured, along with many others. Lots of people were in need of God's love at that point, but to my great surprise, God spoke to me and I heard. I could not imagine that God would choose, then call me, and assign me some role in His work, but he did—just like Paul who got struck while he was trying to get to Damascus, I got struck on my way to Damascus.

I found myself helping the others being held captive—finding food for some, praying with others, letting them cry or get angry. I did not know what to do or how to do it when I saw so many people hungry and hurting. So I made up a prayer that has become my daily prayer ever since: "Lord, here are my hands, my heart, my mind and my mouth. I give them to you do to your work, and I'll try to stay out of your way." To my great surprise, he heard my prayer and accepted my offer.

When we got our freedom, people said that they thought I was a minister or psychologist, because my pastoral work was so helpful. I was amazed because I did not know what I was doing.

When I got home from Beirut, I could not deny that God had chosen me. I could not reject that call. Impossible as it may have seemed, God had reached out to me. Perhaps God felt about me during my time in Beirut just as he felt about the five thousand he once fed in the gospel: Jesus' heart was moved with pity for them because they were troubled and abandoned, like sheep without a shepherd (Matthew 9:36). Whatever happened, it was the first stage of what has led me to become a priest.

When I returned to my home parish of St. Ann's in Ashland, Virginia, I began to work in the parish as a Eucharistic minister, a lector, a cantor, and religious education teacher. Eventually, I headed the Rite of Christian Initiation of Adults program and then the Confirmation program. I could not stop growing in serving God's people because I heard God's call to do so. Then I began to raise handicapped foster children and got involved in other community services.

As time went on, I found that, with the help of several parish priests, I needed to exchange my vocation and many avocations of serving God's people. So I gave up my *vocation* as a college professor and accepted my *avocation* as my new vocation. I was forty-eight years old.

I am so grateful that God has made known his work for me. It was certainly not what I wanted at the time—or even expected. And it caused me to become someone entirely different from what I had planned and hoped for.

I didn't get what I wanted. I got what I needed. And in accepting it, I found out that it was exactly what I really wanted. How wonderful that I had to be knocked off my horse in order to hear his call, just like St. Paul.

Fr. Charles L. Breindel   *Danville, Virginia*

Guiding My Faltering Footsteps

In 2004, I was received into the Catholic Church during the Easter Vigil. This was the end of an almost 40-year spiritual journey, as I had first "received instruction," as it was then called, in the 1960s, and had then, through circumstance and life events, gone through periods of atheism and sixteen years of being a Quaker.

I am fifty-seven years old now, and have had quite an eventful life one way and another. I had certainly sinned as much as the next person, and possibly more! During my RCIA classes, the prospect of having to make my first confession before being received began to seem a bigger and bigger hurdle. In fact, it was almost insurmountable. I prayed about it, I talked about it, I read about it, I agonized over it.

In the month before Easter I started seeing a nun for *counseling*. Of course, my confession was a major topic. At her suggestion, I made an appointment to make my confession to the prior of the friary where we would meet. I knew him slightly by sight, but more by reputation. He is known to be wise, kind, and close to God. Even my parish priest, when he heard of my plans, said "Oh, nothing but the best then?"

The appointed day was the Tuesday of Holy Week. My sponsor came with me for moral support, and we attended Mass together at the friary beforehand. I was a complete bundle of nerves. I had read up on the sacrament of reconciliation and how it is now celebrated. I knew it was going to be *open*—that is, face-to-face, which felt okay. I had had a quick preliminary meeting with the prior, so he was aware of my situation and my nervousness.

It was (from my point of view) a disaster. I doubt if it even lasted ten minutes—remember, I had over fifty years of sinning to confess—and I sobbed the whole time. He listened, he asked no questions, he offered no advice. He gave me absolution and then just left the room, leaving this sobbing mess behind looking at a huge crucifix on the wall!

Yes, I did feel forgiven by and reconciled with God, but that was all. This priest, famed apparently for his compassion and warmth, had left me feeling traumatized and convinced that he was personally disgusted by me. This impression, which I am sure must be wrong, seemed to be further confirmed when I saw him later and he appeared to scuttle out of the way before I had a chance to say "hello".

At this point, quite understandably, you might be thinking, "Hey, hang on here—this isn't exactly an inspirational story about the priesthood," and you would be right. But that was the background. The real story starts now.

A few weeks after Easter, I felt I needed to go to confession again. I didn't want to go to my parish priest, and I certainly didn't want to return to the prior. In the end I just phoned around several churches and chose the one where the confession times that day suited me. This time I went with no expectations except to be absolved. I was an anonymous penitent going to an anonymous priest. And this time it took place within a *closed* confessional, where we could not see each other.

But what a difference. This priest, who I later came to know as Father Paul Connelly of English Martyrs Church, Strood, England, welcomed me and reached out to me with understanding and humanity. He helped me look at the reasons for my sins, how they had affected my relationship with God, and examine ways I might try to avoid committing these sins in the future. It was exactly the experience I had hoped for the first time—not only did I receive absolution, but also acceptance, kindness, advice and healing. I left that confessional renewed and encouraged.

Since then, I am happy to say, Father Paul has become my regular confessor and spiritual director, a true *companion* on my spiritual journey. He hasn't had it easy I have to admit, but fortunately we both consider that I was led to him by God, and as I often tell him, "God will give you the strength you need!"

I don't want to *sanctify* him, and he wouldn't want that either. I am sure that there are many priests out there who have his qualities—I just haven't met them yet. But Father Paul is, to me, God's representative, and as such I have been able to see through him how God accepts me, loves me just exactly as I am, is always ready to listen and forgive and won't give up on me whatever I do. At times it has been a *battle*, with Satan appearing to get the upper ground; but Father Paul has made it abundantly clear that whatever is going on in my life, I must never be afraid to go to him and tell him the worst, and be assured that he (and therefore God) will never reject me whatever I have done.

Through his wise counsel I am able finally to work on areas of my life which have caused me untold misery over the years, such as my need to be *perfect* and the fear of rejection if I'm not. When I can grasp it (and some times are easier than others!), it just blows my mind that God can love me so much, just because He created me.

I never knew my natural father, but now I have the best Father anyone could ever have. One who knows me, loves me unconditionally and one who wants me to spend eternity with Him. A Father who will never let me down, will listen patiently to all my troubles, who forgives His erring daughter again and again.

All this and much more I am learning, thanks to the wonderful priest my Heavenly Father sent into my life to guide my faltering footsteps towards Him. I am a toddler in the spiritual life, and my Father, realizing this, gave me Father Paul to help me, to steer me onto the right path, to pick me up when I fall over, and to haul me back in when I try and run away. He has been an inspiration to me, and I hope this story will be an inspiration to others.

Freya Marshall   *Chatham, Kent, England*

Convinced of God's Love

In 2001, my thirteen-year marriage ended suddenly in a very painful and devastating divorce. Adding to my sorrow was the fact that everyone I had trusted and thought would be supportive and sympathetic quickly disappeared into the woodwork the minute they heard about the divorce. This left me even more bewildered and overwhelmed. Nobody wanted to hear anything about it or talk about it. Suddenly I was an untouchable, left to fend for myself. I felt completely abandoned by everyone, including God.

One night, in the fall of 2003, after two years of trying to deal with my confusion, anger, and hopelessness by myself, I felt I just couldn't take it anymore. I seriously began to consider taking my own life to end the crushing pain and loneliness. But then something inside urged me to try reaching out to someone one last time.

I racked my brain for the name of a person I thought would be willing to listen and help me through this ordeal. Then I remembered Father Patrick Beidelman, a young priest who had been an associate pastor at my parish for the first few years after his ordination. He had been given his own pastorate in 2001, just before I learned that my marriage was going to end, and was now living in a small town nearly two hours from my home in Indianapolis.

Father Patrick and I had served together on the parish liturgy committee, and I remembered him as being friendly, optimistic, and always willing to help others. For him, life was an adventure, not an exile, and he was utterly convinced of God's love and care for every single person. I remembered how, no matter how rotten a day I may have been having, it was impossible to stay in a bad mood around Father Patrick. I hadn't been in touch with him much in the three years since he left my parish, though, and I was afraid he might regard it as an intrusion and a burden if I contacted him. Since I couldn't think of anyone else to try and still had his e-mail address, I went for broke and typed a long e-mail message, pouring out my heart to him. I sent it off without much hope of a response.

A few days later, however, I received an answer from Father Patrick that began with these words, "First of all, my door and e-mail box are always open to you. You are my friend, and in my definition, friends listen to each other in the good times and in the crappy ones, too." He continued with many encouraging and comforting words, and some sensible advice thrown in to boot. I was overjoyed and very relieved to know that I had at least one friend in the world who was willing to stick by me in my darkest hour.

This compassionate priest's brief message was like the first ray of spring sunlight to come through the clouds at the end of a long, hard winter. He encouraged me to keep in touch with him regularly, and offered to be a sounding board anytime I needed to get something off my chest. I accepted his offer and was very grateful that this person, whom I hadn't seen or spoken with for so long, was willing to do this for me—especially since I'm rather melancholy and insecure by nature. Since then, there have been many times when Father Patrick has kindly but firmly pulled me back from the edge of despair and depression. He has always done it with honesty, compassion, gentleness, and a good deal of humor, never showing any sign of exasperation or irritation.

Father Patrick and I have continued our e-mail correspondence for over a year now and have grown to be good friends as a result. He has become a spiritual big brother to me, and he reminds me of the Eastern Orthodox icons of the Blessed Virgin Mary called Hodegetria, *She Who*

Shows the Way. He is always pointing away from himself and towards Christ, encouraging me by word and example to focus upon Jesus, to trust in His love, and to follow Him.

Scripture tells us to remember those who speak the word of God to us and to consider their lives and to imitate their faith. Father Patrick is a caring, gentle, wise man who has become, much to his embarrassment, I daresay, my hero and role model. I know he's not perfect, as none of us is, but I see him actively and faithfully working to cultivate a simple, ingenuous, childlike spirit. He trusts God in every circumstance and is always looking for the joy and peace in difficult situations without denying the pain or sadness that may be there.

This dedicated priest never misses an opportunity to reassure me of God's merciful and never-ending love. It is my sincere prayer and hope that by imitating Father Patrick's faith I too, who am even more flawed and graceless, can nurture within myself his same joyful, trusting, childlike spirit that is centered completely on Christ and shared with others around me.

Father Patrick is a true inspiration for me and I'm sure he is for countless others as well. He's a true joy, and his friendship is my greatest treasure on this earth. His act of kindness in responding to that first e-mail made a huge difference in my life. I thank God every day for Father Patrick's presence in my life and for his vocation as a priest. I know that this wonderful priest keeps me in his prayers and, especially when things get tough, I draw tremendous comfort and strength from that. I pray, too, that one day soon, whenever I am asked the question, "How are you today?" I will be able to answer as Father Patrick invariably does. With much confidence and sporting as big a grin as he possesses, he says, "I'm blessed!"

Linda Pitcher   *Indianapolis, Indiana*

The Keys to a Vast Treasure

In the mid-1980s, Bible study suddenly became the *in thing,* and I was often invited by my friends to join non-denominational scripture study groups. These invitations made me feel uneasy. I was turned off by all the talk of being "born-again" and annoyed by people who constantly quoted scripture to support their opinions.

Finally, to stop them from pestering me, I said, "A priest at Saint Theresa Parish (Palatine, Illinois) has a Bible study group. Saint Theresa is my home parish so I am going to that one!"

My thought was that if I was going to be pressured into being part of the *Bible study craze,* it might as well be in a Catholic setting. That was a less than noble motive for studying the Bible, but, in dealing with me, the Holy Spirit seems to have a sense of humor.

It only took one class for me to be *hooked.* Father William P. Welsh had me hanging onto his every word. He interwove history, culture and his knowledge of the geography of the Holy Land into his lessons on the books of the New Testament. We learned how the Gospels of Matthew, Mark, Luke, and John reflected their personalities and talents. This was fascinating stuff!

Like any good teacher, Father Welsh used props, pictures, current newspaper articles, videos, slides, and his lively presentation to hold our interest. He told stories from his many trips to the Middle East to clarify and explain the background of the scripture passage. He even shared stories from his seminary days.

Father Welsh encouraged us to contribute relevant information. We often vied with one another in our efforts to bring an interesting article, book, or even a challenging question to class. Father answered all of our questions patiently, kindly, and with a sense of humor.

We laughed, we wondered, and sometimes we got misty-eyed. Father once compared our crying out to God, our heavenly Father, as being like a lost child crying out for his mother in the department store. All of us mothers in the group could relate to that. Scripture became alive and meaningful for our everyday lives and not just something to hear on Sunday morning at Mass.

Our group called itself "Father Welsh's Thursday Morning Women's Bible Study." He also had a Bible class for couples in the evening and another Bible study class for young singles. Father was very pleased that several people met their future spouses at that class, and some good Catholic marriages resulted.

Father Welsh gave us clear and confident explanations, but he never hesitated to mention if scripture scholars could not come to an agreement about the meanings of some passages. He had an honest, humble, "we are all learning this together" approach that was very appealing. I quickly lost my cynical attitude. I dusted off the Bible that I had used at Mundelein College, Chicago. The Lord had *tricked* me into becoming religious again, and I was so grateful to Him.

The good news (pun intended) is that even when Father Welsh was transferred to another parish in the Archdiocese of Chicago, he continued to have his many Bible study classes at his new church. Even now, in retirement, he teaches two Bible study classes every week.

My family and I have become friends with Father Welsh and have stayed in touch with him for over twenty years. We are just some of the hundreds of people who have had their faith renewed and refreshed by Father William P. Welsh's teaching, preaching, and celebration of the sacraments.

And no, I still can't quote scripture, chapter and verse, but I have been given the keys to a vast treasure: the books of the Bible. I have grown in my knowledge and love of Jesus. For this and everything you have done for me and my family, I thank you, Father Welsh!

Jacqueline M. Leo   *Palatine, Illinois*

What If?

Back in the 1980s, Father Bell was the pastor of St. Roch's of Flat Rock, Michigan. Besides being a priest, he was a father figure—someone you could talk to, even when faced with a difficult problem. When I started experiencing weakness, dizziness, palpitations, and tachycardia (a rapid heart rate), I was scared. The symptoms would come and go, and the doctors said I was having panic attacks. I didn't accept that diagnosis though, because by nature I had a calm disposition until the symptoms flared up.

There were times when the symptoms would strike and I was convinced I was going to die. Father Bell, prayer teams, and friends prayed over me for healing, and I believe that helped me a great deal. I also went to Father Bell for spiritual counseling, and was very nervous as I blurted out what was happening to me and how I felt. As he listened, he just kind of sat back in his chair and smiled. There was a sparkle in his eyes, and I knew I was in for a challenge of some sort.

"What if?" he asked. I must have had that "Excuse me?" look on my face as he continued. "What if you were to die. What do you believe would happen? What does your faith tell you?" We talked a bit and prayed, and some of the tension left me. The Sunday after Father Bell and I met, I was surprised when his homily was on: "What if?" After Mass he came up to me and with a twinkle-eyed look said, "You know who that homily was for, don't ya?" I replied with a smile, "Oh, yeah."

After that I actually felt better. When I experienced symptoms, I developed the attitude of, "So what?" and waited for them to pass. Eventually they came further apart, but a few years later the symptoms started coming frequently again. This time the doctors had a diagnosis though: I have Graves disease.

Throughout his pastorate at St. Roch's, Father Bell had classes on spiritual growth for his parishioners. When I decided to become a member of the Franciscan family as a secular, Father Bell was supportive and even came to my profession in 1988. I will always remember this special priest for his wonderful support and powerful prayers.

Clara T. Falzone, SFO   *Southgate, Michigan*

A Witness of Grace

In 1999 we moved to Columbus, Ohio, where we became members of St. Philip the Apostle Parish. One Saturday evening during Mass, our pastor, Father Connolly, had some sad news to tell us after he finished his homily. He told us that a dear parishioner, Mr. Leitwein, had passed away. It was clear that this gentleman had been a great help to the parish, and was a beloved friend to Father Connolly. His passing was deeply felt.

As Mass ended, Father Connolly came to the foot of the altar as usual, except this time he stayed there and extended his arms in prayer. It seemed to me that he was giving his friend to God. Then, as he turned to process out of the church, we saw tears streaming down his cheeks. To me this was a witness of grace. It reflected the grace Father Connolly possesses to love our fellow man, and the grace he had that said to Jesus, "I hold these people in my heart." I can't think of anything greater than a parish priest as humble and grace-filled as Father Connolly.

Phillip J. Campbell   *Roseville, California*

He Brought So Much Grace

Monsignor Edmond McGrath was ordained almost sixty-eight years ago. The members of Holy Rosary Parish in Moxee City, Washington, were blessed to have him as their pastor for twenty years. Since his *retirement* in 1997, he continues to reside at Holy Rosary, serves at Mass and keeps an eye on all of us.

Monsignor McGrath was a devoted pastor, a true shepherd watching over his flock. On Sunday mornings, he could almost always be found outside the church doors greeting the parishioners as they came in for Mass. Hospital and nursing home visits were part of his daily ritual. He said it was his job to be there when his people needed him.

We had only been members of the parish for a few years when my father died. None of the priests who had known my parents were available to officiate at his funeral service. His service had passed through a succession of priests, and on the day of the funeral, we still had no idea who would be officiating. We had been guided through my mother's death and funeral six years earlier by a young priest who was close to my parents and my handicapped brother Freddie. In comparison, we were expecting a rather impersonal, cold service conducted by a priest who had never spoken to any of us.

As the doors of St. Paul's Cathedral opened on that cold, dreary February morning, we heard that familiar strong Irish voice of Father McGrath! A friend had told him that my dad was being buried that day. I hadn't thought to call him because I knew he was suffering from a severe case of bursitis, but there he was…ready to assist at the Mass. I will always be grateful for the warmth and comfort that his presence gave us that day.

Ten years later, on another cold Sunday morning in February, he announced to the congregation that he would be cutting the homily short as, he said, my brother Freddie was "slipping away" that morning. Again, I hadn't expected him to come because he had two Masses scheduled that morning. When my friend called him, there was no hesitation. He made the time to come to us in the short time between the Masses. And once more, he brought so much grace and comfort with him. It meant so much to us that he cared enough to be there for us.

Kathleen M. Fredrick   *Moxee City, Washington*

How Do You Know?

I feel that I owe, in part, my very existence to the intervention of a priest some thirty-eight years ago. A year after giving birth to their fourth son in their first four years of marriage, my mother asked a priest about going on birth control. The priest gave my mother permission for a year.

The next year, when she returned for permission again to St. Alphonsus Liguori Church in San Leandro, California, she encountered a different priest. This time an elderly priest, whom she didn't know, pointedly posed this question: "How do you know you are not preventing a special child from being born?"

This question nagged at her heart, and in the end, she decided to place it in God's hands according to His will. That's when I was conceived.

Now, at moments like this, I look towards heaven and say a little thank-you prayer to that priest, whose name I do not know; and to God for my very existence, and for all priests who have the courage to promote the authentic teachings of the Church.

Carolyn D. Susin   *Martinez, California*

I Still Hear His Voice

I was not born or raised a Catholic but my husband, Mark, was. He usually went to church by himself because I was uncomfortable with the unfamiliarity of the Mass. However, that changed one day when he decided to try a new church, St. Mary's, in Vancouver, British Columbia, Canada. A friend he worked with had suggested he go there, and I decided to join him.

With his Irish accent, Father Vincent Travers welcomed all sinners, because only sinners came to St. Mary's Church. I never felt as important as I did when I heard him preach. He related problems of present, everyday life to passages from the Bible, and I felt as if he was speaking to me personally. Before long I was going to church every Sunday, and was attending RCIA classes. At Easter of 1999, I officially became a Catholic.

Father Vincent is a Dominican priest who has served in Iran, Canada, the United States, Portugal, Trinidad, Tobago, and Ireland. His experiences have been varied. He has written four books: *Dancing with Life*, *In Tune with Life*, *In Touch with God*, and *On Song with God*. He also has a web site (www.vincenttravers.org) that he created to keep people close to God even if they don't go to church.

Father Vincent loves the *Abba Father* with his whole heart and passes that love to everyone he meets. I can still hear his voice when I read his books. I was very blessed to have met this wonderful man of God.

Shirley A. Archambault   *New Westminster, British Columbia, Canada*

My Friend, Father Ed

I have worked with missions and missionary groups for twenty-five years, and my greatest joy was to become acquainted with many fine priests and kindly souls. People are so hungry for God, and so many good priests have given their lives to bring their flocks to God, knowing that each soul makes a difference.

I met Father Ed Karlowicz, CR, twelve years ago at St. John Cantius in Chicago, Illinois. I had just begun attending Mass at St. John's when Father Phillips announced from the pulpit that the associate, Father Ed, was in the hospital. My friend and I didn't really know him then, but I thought, "What a great way to get to know him—we can visit him."

So we went to see him every other day and got to know him. The very first night we visited, he had no idea who we were, only that we were parishioners. As providence would have it, the phone rang just as we came in the door.

Father Ed answered, "Hi, Father Frank, I have visitors, wanna talk to them?" and he handed me the phone.

I said, "Hi, Father, this is Sue, and I have Melanie with me." And I handed Father Ed the phone back. That was our introduction.

We visited a short while, and when the conversation lapsed we asked to pray the rosary with him. He loved the rosary, and it became a standard practice to pray the rosary together whenever we visited him.

Just a few weeks later, my own dear father became ill with lung cancer that took his life. For the entire duration of his illness, Father Ed visited him every week even though it was a forty-mile trip each way. My father, long away from the Catholic Church, returned to the Faith through the hands of Father Ed.

Father Ed spent many hours trying to teach me Polish, and I wish I had been a better student. He taught me a Polish song that I remember well because I love to sing.

After the new order was formed, Father Ed was transferred to St. Hyacinth's. I went to see him there, but about one year after he was transferred his health quickly deteriorated. I visited him at the hospital and then at the nursing home near St. Hyacinth's where he was living. He sometimes administered the sacraments, such as confession and last rites, to those of his little flock there.

Visiting him was always a joy and a great learning experience. He told me so many things about the joys of priesthood, the life of a parish priest, and how to be a better Christian. He also expressed the great love he had for the Blessed Mother, for Poland, and for his flock.

During his final hospital stay his sister called me to say that Father Ed was in a coma. She said he would be taken off of the respirator the following morning.

Even though Father Ed's sister had told me that his doctor had asked that he have no visitors other than family, instead of going home after work, I headed for the hospital. His family led me into his intensive care room and shortly after that they went home. I stayed and quietly sang to him the song he had taught me, and, as was our habit during our visits, I started to pray the rosary.

During the rosary, he began to mouth the words of the Hail Marys with me. By the end of the rosary, Father Ed was awake. We spoke for a few moments, and he was tired, so I soon headed home, knowing that the Blessed Mother had most certainly intervened for him. The next day, his sister called again to say they had removed the respirator and that Father Ed was breathing on his own.

About a month later, he had gone to dialysis, as he had to do three times each week, but this time he did not return. Sadly, Father Ed had a heart attack while on the dialysis machine and passed away on September 5. The date was already an important day for me because a couple of years before, on September 5, I had lung cancer removed that should have killed me. I couldn't help feeling that somehow, through his prayers, Father Ed had helped me to survive my illness, later dying himself on that very date. Perhaps it was coincidence, but I felt it deeply, just the same.

I know he is praying for us, and I thank him for the fine example he gave to all who knew him.

Susan E. Gorski   *Naperville, Illinois*

A Special Mass

Father Brian Flanagan first visited my husband and me in November of 1998 when he was a newly ordained priest assigned to our church (St. Paul of the Cross in North Palm Beach, Florida). At the time, my husband, Rocco, was slowly dying from congestive heart failure. This thoughtful priest had noticed my husband's name on our church sick list and called to ask if he could visit us in our home. My husband was truly comforted by this priest's concern and compassion, and for me his regular visits seemed like personal visits from Our Lord, Jesus.

One Wednesday at the beginning of January in 1999, Father Brian called to say that when he came to visit on Friday he wanted to celebrate Mass with us. I was stunned and told him I didn't think there would be enough time for me to invite friends. Father Brian replied that it was not necessary to call friends—that it would be perfect with just the three of us. So, on Friday, Father Brian, Rocco, and I gathered together for Mass in our home, and it was beautiful.

A week later, Rocco died. The Mass that Father Brian had celebrated in our home on that memorable Friday was Rocco's last Mass on earth. It prepared him to return home to Our Lord, and was so very special. Father Brian is now the pastor at St. Patrick Church in Palm Beach Gardens, Florida, and will always remain close to my heart.

Clare C. Andriello-Trosclair   *Palm Beach Gardens, Florida*

Two Guardian Angels

It was a beautiful summer day in the mid-1980s. My husband, Tom, our two sons and I were on our way to our St. Patrick's Day parish picnic in Terre Haute, Indiana. Just prior to arriving at the picnic site, which was on the edge of town on a rural road, our station wagon caught fire. We were very dismayed because we had just spent over four hundred dollars on car repairs the previous day.

We pulled to the side of the road and quickly got out of the burning car with no injuries. My teenaged son, David, carried my severely handicapped son, Billy, at a dead run from the burning car to a homeowner's front yard. Before we could stop him, he ran back to the burning station wagon and removed Billy's wheelchair. He put himself in extreme danger for his brother.

Meanwhile, people from our parish were driving by and saw us in need. Some kind soul called 911, and soon the fire department was there to put the fire out. About this time, Father Todd Riebe, the priest who was helping our parish priest, Msgr. Larry Moran, came along. He got out of his car and was very concerned about us. Father Todd drove us home in his car, and then returned for our son's wheelchair. We were very grateful for his kindness.

A few hours later some people from the parish knocked on our door. They had picnic lunches for us, and also had five hundred dollars in cash to help us buy another car. Father Riebe had collected this money at the church picnic in less than two hours. We were absolutely flabbergasted at this outpouring of love and concern, and amazed that this caring priest had gone out of his way to do this for us.

Father Riebe has since moved on to other churches across the state, but we remember him fondly and keep him in our prayers. We truly had two guardian angels that day: Our oldest son, David, who helped his brother Billy, and Father Todd, who was so compassionate in helping us physically and spiritually.

Bonnie L. Born   *Terre Haute, Indiana*

Our Spiritual Link

My story takes place in 2001, and is about a very special priest who lives far away from where I live in Georgia. His name is Father Jeddie Brooks, and he is the priest at St. Patrick's Church in Monson, Massachusetts.

My roommate and dearest friend had been diagnosed with cancer and, although we were both disabled, I was taking care of her because she was confined to a hospital bed. One night I put her name on prayer lists all over the internet, and one of them was Father Jeddie's St. Peregrine novena page for those with cancer.

This dear, dear priest took us under his wing and called us, wrote to us, sent us books, and literally was our spiritual link during the seven months that my roommate lived with the cancer. He even called to check on me the day she died. Amazingly, he did all this while his own father was battling cancer.

Father Jeddie's love and support led me to the Catholic Church, and I became a member of St. John's Church in 2003. This compassionate priest and friend was my sponsor. He continues to call and write, and to this day is a dear friend to me.

Debbie B. Oliver   *Valdosta, Georgia*

Three Priests

Though I hold a deep admiration for each man who has dedicated himself to following God's call to the priesthood, there are three in particular who have impacted my life as a Catholic. I was raised a Protestant and therefore had no understanding about the Church or the priesthood until I was grown. These three priests have touched my life in a special way, and I would like to pay tribute to them.

Father Austin Ernstes, a Franciscan, came to my parish, St. Helen Catholic Church in Portales, New Mexico, early on in my journey in the faith. Father Austin was not only rather elderly, but he was afflicted with severe physical problems. It was even difficult for him to walk because of shortness of breath.

At one particular Holy Thursday Mass, the members of the parish council, on which I served, were chosen to go to the altar and be seated in order to have their feet washed. I was stunned and humbled beyond words when Father Austin began washing our feet. When he came to me, kneeling at my feet, I wanted to tell him that he should sit and let me wash his instead. After he washed and anointed my feet, he gazed at me with a look of the love and compassion of Christ, and I was left with a profound sense of peace.

Father Ivo Zirchelback was also a Franciscan. When he arrived at our parish on December 31, 1988, we all knew he had leukemia. He never let that interfere with his duties, however, and though he was not well-liked in the parish by many since he followed a young, charismatic pastor, he remained loving and giving.

One day, when I was serving as an extraordinary minister of Communion, I was in the sacristy when he came in the door. I greeted him, and as one often does, asked how he was. He replied that he really wasn't feeling well because he had fallen in the shower. He proceeded to conduct the liturgy and said nothing about his problem from the pulpit.

I later learned that during the next Mass he mentioned his discomfort and agreed to sit on a stool at the altar. After that Mass, he went to the hospital, only to learn that he had fractured his hip. It was almost unbelievable that he had overcome the pain that many of us can only imagine, in order to continue serving the Lord. At the end of his life, Father Ivo was in a nursing home and I was privileged to be with him when he died. He had absolutely no fear but only a deep, continual faith in God.

Another priest who has touched my life is Father Carlos Chavez. He came to Clovis, New Mexico, as a very young man to be pastor of Sacred Heart Parish on January 1, 1989. He came into what would be a difficult situation for any man.

Father Carlos was to be the first Hispanic and non-Franciscan pastor of Sacred Heart Parish. His immediate command from the archbishop was to close the parish school, which was a very unpopular decision with most of the congregation. He was troubled with personal problems also—those of rather poor health and being the basic financial supporter of his father who lived in another city. He was serving in the National Guard as a chaplain, probably for additional income to send to his father.

After a term in Clovis, on May 30, 1982, he was transferred to the cathedral in Santa Fe where he served as associate pastor for a time. He came back to our parish on July 1, 1994, in worse health than before. Father Carlos is the most loving, compassionate, faith-filled priest I have ever known. Sometimes during the sacrament of reconciliation I have felt that he has the wisdom of Solomon. I feel truly blessed that we have him as our pastor.

Other priests have been instrumental in my walk in faith, but these three stand out as the most notable.

Virginia Schmuck   *Portales, New Mexico*

In Remembrance

The following is a homily given by Father Jeremy Myers at Msgr. John T. Gulczynski's funeral Mass on July 6th, 2004. As you will see, it is a wonderful testimony and witness of how many lives this special monsignor touched.

Father Jeremy writes all of his own homilies, and while he was giving this one at the very large and deep St. Thomas Aquinas Church, you could almost hear a pin drop. What is even more amazing about Father Jeremy is that he doesn't read his homilies, he just talks. He is currently a pastor at St. Mary's Catholic Church in Sherman, Texas. I believe that Msgr. John would be very proud of how Father Jeremy is leading and guiding the sheep of his flock.

In Remembrance of Monsignor John T. Gulczynski

2 Kings 2.1,6-14

Bishop Grahmann, Father Libone, fellow priests, nieces and nephews of Msgr. John, parishioners of St. Thomas Aquinas, friends all, grace and peace be with you.

We are told that when the great Hebrew leader Moses passed from this life to the next, the Israelites wept for thirty days, so great was their grief at his passing. Today, we also know grief, for we have lost a great leader. The Hebrew Scriptures also tell us of Moses that, "Since then no prophet has arisen in Israel like Moses." We could say much the same. There will never be another like Msgr. John.

"Extraordinary" is a word that, by its very nature, should not be used often. For most causes and on most days, the word "ordinary" is sufficient. Today, we use the word "extraordinary" because we gather to remember someone who was not ordinary. I don't recollect anyone ever saying Msgr. John was an ordinary person. He was extraordinary or, as we often say, "one of a kind." We were the ones blessed by his extraordinary life.

And like another great Biblical figure who also bore his name, John the Baptist, Msgr. John was a person of convictions. Someone said the other day that Father John never took "no" for an answer. A person of conviction never does. Monsignor was like a ship with sails set for port and he did not waver on the seas. His course was set for the other shore.

The nineteenth century German poet Heinrich Heine once traveled through Europe. One day he stood with a friend before the grand Cathedral of Amiens, France. "Tell me, Heinrich," the friend wondered aloud, "Why can't people build buildings like this anymore?" Heinrich is said to have answered his friend in this way. He said, "In those days, people had convictions. We moderns have opinions. And," said the poet, "it takes more than opinions to build a cathedral."

He spoke well. It does take more than opinions to build a cathedral. It takes conviction. We sit beneath this splendid nave in this exquisite church, not because Msgr. John had opinions, but because he had convictions. He built not only this church, but also this parish, from the ground up, and it was built brick by brick by one man's convictions that such a place could be and would be, and fifty-two years later we see what a man with vision and conviction can do.

I used to think it an odd combination, Msgr. John, of Polish heritage, in a predominately Italian parish. But as another churchman of Polish descent with the name John Paul would prove in Rome many years later, this Polish man won the hearts of the Italians and they claimed him as their own. Yet, I think his parishioners called him "Father John", not only because of a fond affection, which was true, but also because the name "Gulczynski" had a most difficult time rolling off of Italian lips.

As I said, Monsignor had conviction about many things. Another of his favorites was St. Thomas Aquinas School. He brought the Sisters of the Holy Family of Nazareth to administer and teach in the school, and built them a convent on the grounds that would house eighteen nuns, a feat beyond our comprehension. Again, it takes conviction to build on such a grand scale.

You may recall in Georges Bernano's book, *Diary of a Country Priest*, the priest tells the reader, "This morning I prayed hard for my parish, my first and perhaps my last, since I ask no better than to die here. My parish!" The priest then says, "The words cannot even be spoken without a kind of soaring love."

Msgr. John had that kind of "soaring love" for this parish. It was not his first—that was Holy Family in Vernon—nor his second, which was Sacred Heart Cathedral here in Dallas, but it was the one he loved the most, and like the country priest, he prayed hard for his parish. I never saw him leave this church after saying Mass without taking time to kneel in this sanctuary and remember to God these, his people.

Msgr. John also asked no better than to die here. That wish was granted him when Bishop Tschoepe honored him as Pastor Emeritus upon his retirement in 1989. This was his home. Msgr. John was the indisputable leader of this parish for thirty-seven years, a near unprecedented tenure in our time, and an impressive indicator again of his conviction.

As most of you know, countless new priests would train under Msgr. John during his many years here at St. Thomas Aquinas. In some ways, it was boot camp for us—complete with discipline, decisiveness, and a drill sergeant. He wanted those who trained under him to have the same strength of character and conviction that he did. If some of us marched to our own drummer, he would summon us back with his well-known line, "We don't do that here."

I don't know how many assistants trained under him. I have heard something like thirty, which, when you do the math, is about one a year. Imagine having to train a new recruit every year. Again, it is a job for the strong and the assured. I was the last. Like the baby of the family, I am often reminded by my predecessors how easy I had it. I would simply say that even after thirty assistants, Monsignor was still a man of conviction and not a man of opinions. He expected the best from all of us and, in the process, he taught us to expect the best of ourselves.

We learned many things from Msgr. John—how to say Mass, how to lead, and how to follow. We also learned not to ride in the same car with Monsignor because he took to the road with the same conviction he took to everything else in life. It took diplomacy and determination on my part to tell Monsignor it would be better if I drove us. It was the only argument I ever won with him, so maybe he really had mellowed by the time I came along.

Sacred Scripture tells us that young Elisha was given a double portion of his mentor, Elijah's spirit when Elijah was taken up into the heavens in a whirlwind. I am sure Msgr. John wished his assistants the same favor, but I know that I, for one, will never be his equal, much less have double his spirit.

Msgr. John loved everything about being a priest. He was ordained younger than Church law allowed at the time and he began a life of priestly ministry that would span over the next six decades. During that time he would serve as chancellor of the diocese for ten years; serve as a consulter to three bishops here; he would receive a doctorate in canon law from Catholic University of America. Some say he could have been a bishop; I think he found his greatest happiness in simply being pastor of this church.

The great American Jewish writer Chaim Potok described in one of his novels a team of baseball players as "playing like it was the first of the Ten Commandments." Msgr. John approached the priesthood with that same kind of conviction, as if it was the first of the Ten Commandments. It is unimaginable that he would have been anything else. Like John the Baptist, he was ordained in the womb.

Some may ask what Msgr. John was like in private. For those of you who did not get to see him outside these walls, he was everywhere much the same. He was a gentleman. He was generous. He enjoyed people around him and was a gracious host. What did he like? He liked tradition. He loved Christmas. He liked a glass of Louis Jadot wine at meals, not to be confused with Jean Jadot. On special occasions he would have Crown Royal on the rocks.

Let me assure you that Monsignor was also the consummate creature of habit. Every Sunday evening he went to dinner with several priest friends. He went home to Delaware after Christmas and Easter Masses each year. Every summer he went to Rome with his friend

Father Gately. And lunch was always one hour long. You can ask any of his assistants.

I remember when it was just the two of us here. Msgr. John continued to put up on the downstairs bulletin board the weekend assignment of Masses, a routine he had established many years before when there were as many as three assistants here. I mentioned to him one day that there really wasn't any need for him to work out a schedule anymore since we both knew what the other would be doing on weekends. The next Friday the schedule went up as usual. I learned again that is the way we do it here.

To the best of my knowledge, Monsignor feared no one and nothing. Fear simply wasn't in his person. He stayed true to God, to the Church, and to himself, and that didn't leave much room for fear. Not everyone always saw eye-to-eye with Msgr. John, but everyone knew exactly where he stood. As I said, he was a man of conviction, not opinions.

I remember reading once where a famous Nobel Prize recipient was asked a question about his religious affiliation. He answered, "probably Christian." I think it's safe to say that Msgr. John never used the word "probably" in his entire life. There was too much uncertainty and lack of clarity in the word "probably" for Monsignor's tastes.

"He is to be called John." Both Elizabeth and Zechariah were convinced of the rightness of the name for their son. And so it was, even if no other of their relatives bore the name. John is translated, "Yahweh is gracious." I like to think that God was gracious to us when He blessed us with this John. I know I consider my time with Monsignor to be grace.

"What will this child be? Was not the hand of the Lord upon him?" All the neighbors of Zechariah and Elizabeth asked each other. I think that the hand of the Lord also was upon this John as he led us and challenged us. Msgr. John even had the voice of John the Baptist—loud, clear, and confident.

But now the voice that once prayed, that sang, that led us, is still. Even with all the sounds in this church today, it is a quiet place because Msgr. John's voice is no longer heard. It was a gradual fading over the last years as poor health took Msgr. John from us. Then, finally, at an age of almost Biblical proportions, ninety-two, the voice was completely silent.

Holy Writ tells us that God created the heavens and the earth for six days and on the seventh, He rested. It is good for us to know that even the greatest of builders rested. When Augustine preached on the story of creation, he reminded his people that there shall come a time when we ourselves shall become that seventh day. On that day we will be re-plenished and restored by the blessing of God. Augustine says we will be filled by God when He will be all in all.

I like to think that Msgr. John has now arrived at that seventh day. He spent a lifetime turning chunks of clay into something good, something beautiful. His handiwork will stand here for many generations, so well did he build this church, this parish, this people. Now, rest and be still, Monsignor. You have reached the seventh day. It is our prayer that you gaze in peace upon the splendor of God, whom you served so well here below.

Kathy M. Metevier   *Dallas, Texas*

I Love You, Jesus!

I am pastor of St. Joan of Arc Parish Community of Harper County, in the Wichita Diocese of Kansas.

When I was a young priest in 1984, I was celebrating Mass one Sun-day morning at the Christ the King Church in Wichita. I was just getting ready for holy Communion, when I felt someone hugging my knees.

I looked down and there was a young girl around three years of age. She was kissing me and saying, "I love you, Jesus!"

Twenty years later, a young woman introduced herself to me as the young girl who visited me at the altar. She is now a novice of the Immaculate Heart of Mary Sisters. She has assumed the name of Sister Mary Agnes.

Rev. Michael Peltzer   *Harper, Kansas*

Dining with the Bishop

Many years ago I was a seminarian studying for the Diocese of Springfield-Cape Girardeau in Missouri. My bishop during that time was Bernard F. Law, who later became Cardinal Law.

After several years of discernment I determined that the priesthood was not my calling and left the seminary in 1975. I later moved to Memphis, Tennessee, where I met and married my beloved wife Kathleen in 1978. As blessings come when one is open to them, in the first four years of our marriage we were blessed with three babies.

On one memorable occasion, probably in 1982, Kathleen, the kids, and I were in Glennonville, Missouri, visiting my parents. There was a big celebration that weekend at Mom and Dad's parish, St. Teresa's, and Bishop Law was to be guest of honor at a parish potluck dinner. Somehow Kathleen and I ended up at the very end of the serving line, and, as luck would have it, the only seats left were those directly across the table from the bishop.

So, we sat down with our three little children: a two-year-old, a one-year-old, and a baby. Kathleen, a recent convert to Catholicism, was nervous about sitting across from Bishop Law, but since he was a very gracious man, he made us feel at ease.

Of course, I will admit to my own twinge of awkwardness...after all, one could feel a bit strange dining with one's former bishop after having left the seminary and now with a wife and children. At the conclusion of the meal, however, Bishop Law turned to me, patted me on the arm, and said, "You did good."

Until her death in 2003, Kathleen bragged frequently about that incident. She always claimed that she had received her own personal "ecclesiastical approbation" that night.

Francis R. White   *Memphis, Tennessee*

A Simple Invitation

Back in the late spring of 1986, our pastor at Holy Spirit Parish decided to interview each family that had children who were attending Catholic schools or CCD classes at the parish. Father Davey interviewed hundreds of families over a period of weeks, and by the time the interviews were completed, he was quite hoarse. However, he was so pleased with the results that he decided he would repeat this process at his next assignment, sooner in his tenure than he had done at our parish. It was a great way for everyone involved to meet one-on-one.

After receiving the third call to make an appointment for our interview, I reluctantly scheduled ours. I was on the education committee and served in several other groups at the time, and my husband, Don, was no stranger to the parish either. I felt that Father Davey was already very familiar with us. However, as we spoke during our meeting, he was surprised to learn that my husband, who regularly attended Mass with us, wasn't Catholic. He discovered this when he asked Don why he never went to Communion.

Then Father Davey said, "I have seen you come to church every Sunday for years and just assumed you were Catholic. How would you like to join us and become a full-fledged Catholic? We are gathering a new group for RCIA, which will be starting in September, and I know Sister Bede would love to have you join the class and learn more about our faith."

Don beamed and accepted this gracious, unexpected invitation. Throughout that summer, before classes began, Don, who is an avid reader, turned to reading more and more about our faith. He was very excited and looking forward to the RCIA process.

Sister Bede was a very gentle, elderly person who had converted to our faith when she was in her teen years. Everyone in the parish loved her, including my family. She led the RCIA group through religious instructions, and my husband was received into full communion with the Catholic Church on Easter of 1987. Thank you, Father Davey, for that simple invitation offered at just the right moment in God's time. And thank you, Sister Bede, for your patience and care during the instructional process.

Mary Joan Douglas   *Saginaw, Michigan*

A Minister of Jesus

Father Joseph Ross, M.S., has been a special member of our family for many years.

We have cried together, laughed together, worked together and played together. He is a very humble man, quiet and unassuming. He ran a youth group at La Salette for many years. My children attended his group and learned so much about the Catholic religion and how to be good, but real, people.

Father Joseph was always there for us, and our family was honored to have his guidance. He celebrated joyous occasions with us, and on tragic occasions, he cried with us. He ministered to us just as Jesus would have done, and we entrusted our very souls to him. He was and is a beautiful servant to our dear Lord.

Lynn Y. Francis   *Providence, Rhode Island*

Experiencing God's Love

Some years back we had a priest in our parish who had been ordained in his later years. At this time, we were experiencing some difficulty with our son, and I felt very alone with this problem. Even though we sought all kinds of psychological help, nothing seemed to help.

One morning after a weekday Mass, I approached the priest and asked him if he had time to talk. I think I was probably somewhat belligerent out of frustration with my son. I was probably feeling anxious, too, because I had recently approached another priest and had been told that I shouldn't expect to have things easy and that things were different for kids now, not like when we were younger.

This priest told me kindly that he had the time to talk with me. We both ended up talking and listening to each other—I needed to do both—and even though the problems weren't solved, I experienced God's love through this priest's willingness to take the time to listen to my problems. I don't know how busy he really was that morning, or if he had put other things on hold, but I felt as though he had all the time in the world and that he thought my problems were important enough to warrant his time.

I wish there were more priests like him and I pray for vocations all the time now.

Anne B. Caron   *Hartford, Connecticut*

Converting Father Fisher

There are so many stories I could tell about Father Merle J. Fisher that they could fill a whole book. This priest was born in 1933, was raised in Homedale, Idaho, was professed in the Society of Mary in 1954, and ordained at the National Shrine of the Immaculate Conception in February of 1960. Father Fisher loved God, and everyone He put on earth; rich or poor, good or bad—he loved them all.

We *coffee klatschers* routinely gathered around the dining room table in the rectory after morning Mass at St. Paul's Catholic Church in Nampa, Idaho. This was during the late 1970s and most of the 1980s when Father Fisher was pastor. We discussed various topics of the day, and they weren't always religious. Sometimes they were downright hilarious. We never talked politics in any shape or form, and Father Fisher had no tolerance for gossip. He looked forward to our morning coffee as much as we did.

Oh, what stories he would tell when we were together. One of my favorites was about his neighbors who kept an early morning vigil every day, watching people arrive for Mass. Being Pentecostals, the gentleman and his wife were always trying to convert Father Fisher. They were on a mission to persuade him away from the "evils of Catholicism" out of their "love and concern" as they would say. His usual response was a cheerful invitation to have coffee and talk over any questions they had, and then he would bless them and wish them a happy day.

Once a week this couple would sneak into the church and put anti-Catholic tracts in the hymnals, unaware that they were being observed. Suddenly, a week went by without the tracts, and then two. Then one afternoon Father Fisher had a surprise visit from this good neighbor—he wanted to talk. Thinking it was another conversion attempt but being gracious as always, Father Fisher invited the man into his office, where, of course, the first thing he did was bring his guest a cup of coffee.

The neighbor appeared to be very uncomfortable and ill at ease. Trying to make him feel at home, Father Fisher couldn't resist teasing him a little and asked what his new complaint was against the Church. After a moment or so, the neighbor brought forth a handful of the anti-Catholic tracts, and admitted it was he and his wife who had been placing them in the hymnals. He apologized to Father Fisher and asked for his forgiveness.

In all his years as a priest, this was the first time Father Fisher had heard the confession of such a dedicated opponent as this non-Catholic neighbor. Sensitive to the differences in their respective beliefs, he thanked him for his courage and honesty, and assured him of his forgiveness. Then in a sudden inspiration, he offered a prayer for his neighbor asking for God's forgiveness as well. Father Fisher quietly accepted the *evidence of bad behavior* and slipped the tracks into the trash pail. He never let on that he had known about the tracts all along.

The neighbor had one more surprise for Father Fisher. Could both he and his wife come for instructions in the Catholic faith? Just as Our Lord rejoiced over one penitent sinner, Father Fisher rejoiced in his quiet, humble way over his neighbors' change of heart. But he could no longer resist asking what had brought about this change; what had motivated this visit?

The man explained that it was due to their early morning *Mass watches*. He and his wife had started out by looking at the church-goers with pity, especially the elderly who would come out in Idaho winters at 7:30 in the morning, day after day. One lady in particular got their attention.

There were long, steep steps up to the front doors of the church. Volunteers tried to keep them clear, even with the snow falling. The neighbors watched each day as that particular lady slowly made her way up those long flights of stone steps, often assisted by other parishioners. It made them wonder what it was that kept the people coming out, even in bad weather. That would not have happened in their own church. Curiously, they decided to find out for themselves and quietly went to Mass one morning when Father Fisher was the celebrant. They didn't understand the Mass but did understand the love that radiated in that church. They also knew something quite special was taking place when Father Fisher elevated the Host at the consecration.

The lady he was talking about was a long-time parishioner who Father Fisher and all of us knew. She had never been aware of the power of her quiet devotion to the Mass and the witness it became for others. Father Fisher had been equally unaware of the power of his own witness of great love and devotion as he elevated the Eucharist at each and every Mass. It was God working through him just as He worked through that elderly parishioner. The following year, the neighbors were both confirmed into the holy Catholic Church.

Above all, Father Fisher loved Jesus and His Blessed Mother. His most cherished possession was a statue of the Madonna given to him as a young priest. It went everywhere with him and kept vigil at his bedside. His beloved Madonna was there to comfort and encourage him during his last days in this life at St. Anne's Home in San Francisco. There he was lovingly tended by the Little Sisters of the Poor who had their own stories to tell of how he inspired and enlivened their days and comforted the other terminally ill patients. He never left his wheelchair. His last words to his nurse-in-charge were, "I am ready, Sister, I have my Madonna." Father Fisher died of MLS just after Thanksgiving, 2002.

June R. St. James-Pfouts   *Chapel Hill, North Carolina*

He Needs Some Ice Cream

In 1984, I was a stay-at-home mother raising four children who were ten, nine, seven, and six years old. When my oldest son, Jonathan, turned ten, he became very troubled. One frightening night he tried to stab himself with a kitchen knife. After calming him down and getting him to sleep, I sat up all night praying. I asked Jesus to send me someone to help me raise my children in the faith because I strongly believed that our Catholic faith was what my children needed to get through life, and to get to heaven. At the time, my husband did not share my faith or go to Mass with us. I was feeling very alone, overwhelmed, and scared.

The next day, as I was bringing the children to their catechism classes at St. Anthony Parish, one of our priests, Father Joseph Illo, greeted us and said to my son Jonathan, "You look old enough for my youth group." A few days later Jonathan and my second oldest son, Joey, joined his lively youth group, *Anthony's Angels*.

I began helping Father Joseph, along with the other parent volunteers, and for the first time in my life, I had friends with whom I could pray and share my faith. My sons soon became altar servers, and because the people we met were so nice, my husband began going to Mass with us.

Father Joseph took his youth group on many trips and bike rides. We even learned to ski and climb mountains together. On these trips, we always prayed the rosary, and Father Joseph would tell us angel and saint stories as we sat around the campfire. He also taught me how to pray the Liturgy of the Hours, and I have not missed a day in ten years.

When Jonathan was thirteen years old, he began struggling with adolescence and made some bad choices. One night, the police took him to a behavioral clinic after he had been in a fight and had threatened to commit suicide. My husband stayed home with the younger children, and I followed the police car that was taking Jonathan to the clinic. Before leaving the house, I called Father Joseph and left a message. I didn't know when he would get it though, because he was a vocations director and was seldom home.

The behavior clinic was a frightening place and I could tell it was not good for Jonathan to be there, but the staff would not let me take him home. Then, suddenly, Father Joseph arrived. He talked with Jonathan and calmed him down, and then told the staff, "This boy does not need to stay here. He just needs some ice cream." Surprisingly, they let us go home.

Time and time again Father Joseph has been there for my family and many others during turbulent times. He always helps to calm the storms or ride them out with us in faith.

Jonathan and I went with Father Joseph and the youth group to Rome for World Youth Day in 2000. It was a trip we will never forget. My youngest son, Jeremy, went to Toronto for World Youth Day in 2002, but I was unable to go with him because I was very ill. I had cancer and was given one year to live. During my illness, Father Joseph supported our family with his prayers and friendship, and was a real source of strength to my husband.

I was miraculously healed of cancer through the intercession of Blessed Teresa of Calcutta, and as of this writing, I'm in good health and planning to go to Cologne for World Youth Day with my daughter, Melody.

Since 2000, Father Joseph has been the pastor of St. Joseph Parish in Modesto, California. As soon as he arrived there, he consecrated the large and very active parish to the Immaculate Heart of Mary. He also established perpetual adoration that has flourished so much that it has out-grown the chapel.

I have seen Father Joseph face and overcome many obstacles, large and small, through his incredible faith. He is a courageous priest who is never afraid to preach the whole truth, no matter what it may cost him in suffering or popularity.

Father Joseph may take a day off from the parish from time to time, but in the many years that I have known him, he has never taken one second off from being a priest. I am forever grateful to God for answering my desperate prayer to send someone to help me raise my children in the faith, and for answering my unspoken prayer for a true friend. God really does more for us than we can ask or imagine. My family and our whole parish community are very blessed for knowing Father Joseph as a priest and as a friend.

Debbie A. Greco   *Manteca, California*

My Spiritual Guide

I have an aunt living in St. Georges, Newfoundland, who is a Sister of the Presentation of the Blessed Virgin Mary. In 1989, I visited her when she was celebrating her twenty-fifth jubilee with my father. During our visit, my dad started complaining about a sore chest, and since the weather in Newfoundland was damp, we thought he had the flu and nothing more. One week later, he had a massive heart attack and died. This broke my heart, especially because he had begged me to stay with him, and I didn't because I needed to get back to work, or so I thought.

While I was in Newfoundland, my wrists were excruciatingly sore, but I tried not to complain and ruin the special event. When I returned home I needed to have both of my wrists replaced, as well as three joints in my right hand. Within a short time, I had experienced the loss of my dad, my health, and my job. I was in the Lord's hands.

Thankfully, this is when God brought Father Mazerole into my life. He helped me through this challenging time, and I am not sure what I would have done without this kind, intelligent man. He was easy to approach and a very happy person whom I could talk with for hours and it would seem like only ten minutes had gone by. During walks together, I felt so much at home with him that I was sure he was from heaven itself.

When I first met Father Mazerole, he was a priest at St. Lawrence Parish in Halifax, Nova Scotia. After that he was transferred to Bedford Parish until his death five years ago. I was with Father Mazerole the night he passed away at St. Vincent Guest Home. The room had an unbelievable aura of peace. I miss him so very much, but I am comforted knowing that God has other spiritual beings on earth to guide my footsteps.

Corinne M. Quinlan   *Dartmouth, Nova Scotia, Canada*

Reaching Out

After major surgery in the early 1980s, Jack was taken out of the field as a telephone repairman and placed in a court building. Because of his easy manner and deep faith, some of the police officers he met there felt comfortable talking to him about their problems. One was a young man who was recently widowed, and another one had a wife who was being treated for cancer. Both men grew very close to Jack. They frequently told him what was weighing heavily on them, and he would listen intently. He had a feeling they wanted to return to their Catholic faith, but that they needed help taking that first step.

I'm a man who likes to cook so when he mentioned this to me I said, "Let's get them together with Father Walter. We can all sit down together and have a relaxing dinner, and Father Walter can talk to them." At that time, this priest was assigned to St. John's Parish in Bergenfield, New Jersey.

Not surprisingly, they all came to dinner (Why wouldn't they? I'm a fairly decent chef.). Father Walter D. Cron arrived last and sat with very relaxed body language at the head of the table. While my wife and I served our guests, Father Walter put everyone at ease with his fatherly manner. As the dinner progressed, the officers placed themselves in his confidence and poured their hurts out to him, one page at a time.

As the meal was ending, the widower asked Father Walter if he would hear his confession. They got up from the table and went to a finished room in the basement where they celebrated the sacrament of reconciliation. When they returned to the table, the other man asked to receive the sacrament as well. When they returned, the wife of the second man, the one who was ill, asked to have her confession heard. However, she wasn't Catholic.

Up until this time, she had attended Mass regularly with her husband, and when she asked her pastor if she could receive Communion, the pastor did not permit her to. Because of her illness, though, a lot of red tape was circumvented the night of our dinner. Father Walter heard her confession and anointed her, and we warmly welcomed her into the Catholic Church.

Later, at Mass in her own church, she told her pastor what happened that night. At Communion time she not only received the Eucharist with her husband, but was given the Precious Blood as well. Miraculously, at her next physical she was found to be in full remission.

Father Walter is retired now, but the church continues to be served by people he brought back to the church. It was common for him to reach out to people in ways like this. He had an impact on my life, too, and at my ordination to the diaconate my mother pointed to me and asked Father Walter, "How the heck did he ever become a deacon?" He is a great priest whose influence is felt by many.

Deacon Bob Thomson   *Edgewater, New Jersey*

God's Own Coincidences

It is said that a coincidence is a miracle where God remains anonymous. I am a believer.

Two aircraft touched down in Korea on September 12, 1976, depositing two Americans with two decidedly different tasks.

I had been dispatched from Washington, D.C., much to my displeasure, to help fix a problem in my Air Force unit. Father Sal, fresh from language school, was to begin his missionary career. We met on a bus headed for a remote mission post for a Christmas holiday.

126

Father Sal assisted at midnight Mass, but the frustration due to his limited command of the Korean language was evident. On Christmas morning, the two of us sat at a small table in a chilly rectory kitchen.

Father Sal shared his disappointment, and I asked if he would celebrate a Mass for me in English, since, I confided, I had not got much out of the midnight Mass.

He was delighted! The Mass that we shared was the best experience of Christ entering the world I have ever known.

Our friendship deepened in the year I was in Seoul, Korea, and we shared many adventures. In 1980, he returned to the United States for his first vacation. My wife Marj and I twisted his arm until he agreed to visit us in Maryland and make a Marriage Encounter weekend. We were part of the presentation team. Father Sal had a great weekend and told us he had been considering leaving the priesthood, but the weekend had renewed his call.

He managed to stay in touch with us, and he spent time with our family during his home leaves. Our four children called him our "family chaplain." Little did we know how demanding that task would be.

When I became a permanent deacon in September 1993, Father Sal managed to arrange a visit to attend my ordination. I was thrilled when he vested me.

In the summer of 1994, our five-year-old grandson Edward was close to death as a result of a rare genetic disease. Father Sal, in the United States working on a doctorate, dropped his studies and joined our family. Upon arrival, amid a sea of tears, Father Sal tenderly anointed Edward.

All the adults took turns at Edward's side, including Father Sal, so Edward was never alone. Two nights before Edward died, I was crossing a landing on the second floor of my daughter's home. It was about two a.m. I glanced down. Father Sal was tending to Edward and was changing his diaper. Medicine that Edward was taking created a terrible rash and rawness, and as Father Sal cleaned and dressed that tender bottom, he talked to Edward in low tones, ones I couldn't make out. I recall Edward giggling for one of the last times in his short life. Honestly, I could see Father Sal united with a compassionate Christ.

On a beautiful sun-filled afternoon, Edward took his last breath in his father's arms, with Father Sal and me touching him in prayer. I assisted at a joyous funeral Mass that Father Sal celebrated.

Since then Father Sal has presided at a daughter's wedding, and we attended his silver anniversary Mass. Father Sal himself suffered a serious medical incident which has forced him to the sidelines, but we get together when we can and stay in touch through e-mail and telephone calls. I know I would not be a permanent deacon without Father Sal's prayers, witness, and love.

Not coincidentally, Edward died on my birthday. I had asked my mother in heaven to put in a good word to take Edward home as a birthday present to me, and I'm sure she did. Nothing happens by accident.

Eugene K. Mastrangelo   *North Beach, Maryland*

Four Sons

My mother-in-law lived across the street from St. Paul's Monastery on the south side of Pittsburgh, Pennsylvania. We usually visited her on Saturdays so we could run across the street and go to confession while we were there.

As a parent of teenagers, I often had guilt-ridden thoughts running rampant in my mind while I was waiting in line to go to confession. I would think, "I should not have yelled at him. That's anger. Maybe I shouldn't have grounded him, but should have talked to him first. That's anger and impatience. Maybe I should have..." and the list would go on and on.

This particular day I really needed to see a priest I didn't know because I didn't want to look bad to my parish priest. I felt like telling all the other people in line that even if they had serious sins they should go to the back of the line because I wanted to get in there and get this over with.

The confessor that day was Father Anthony, an elderly Passionist priest. As I began my laundry list of sins about my anger with the boys, he asked, "My dear, how many children do you have?" I answered, "Four sons." With his eyes rolled heavenward, he repeated in a holy whisper, "Four sons."

"Yes, Father Anthony," I responded. Looking into my eyes like I was some kind of hero, he said softly, "You have four sons." Again I said, "Yes, Father Anthony." This time he asked in a tone of voice like he wanted make sure he had it straight. "You have four sons?" "Yes, Father Anthony, four sons."

Then he raised his eyes heavenward again, and with his hands folded he whispered another holy whisper, this time saying, "Thank you Lord for giving this lady four sons." By this time tears were streaming down my face and dripping off my chin, and he kindly passed me the tissues.

Father Anthony was more grateful for my four sons that day than I had been before I talked to him. My heart melted in those next few moments as I had a good cry and felt God's forgiveness. The anger was gone and the priest's holy whispered words, "You have four sons," was all I heard echoing in my heart for the rest of the day.

Praise God for Father Anthony's reminder of what a wonderful gift from God my sons are to me. As I left the confessional, it was my turn to speak in a holy whisper. From the bottom of my heart I whispered, "Thank you, Father Anthony."

Judy V. Krantz   *Tarentum, Pennsylvania*

A True Friend

I believe there are many Catholics who love to tell their stories of positive influences from priests, and, in my own mind, such stories also tell a story about Our Savior.

My first story involved Father Patrick Sullivan, who reunited me with the Church after an absence of ten years. The parish was St. John the Baptist de la Salle in Mission Hills, Calif. Our son was named after him, and it does warm my heart that this tradition probably coincides with many other mothers' heart felt gratitude. God is so good and keeps giving His people gifts. My reuniting with the Church occurred in the 1970s, and that was not the last gift to be given.

Fast forward to Hollywood, 1990—a place and time that sorely needs the Christian message, a city of great disparity between grace and sin, poor and rich, fame and obscurity. A young man, John Palatucci, comes to my office to be my assistant. This is a very different arrangement, for I have always worked for men but have never had a male assistant.

"What did you do over the weekend?" was my new assistant's first personal question to me.

The culture I lived in went against what would be the true answer, that I had spent it around church and family life. My mind reeled for a few moments as I wondered, "Do I keep the door open to a relationship and not be honest, or do I tell the truth?"

Finally, I decided to tell the truth. At least if he were turned off, I would not have to be bothered with his life, which probably revolved around pop music. So I told him the truth.

What a surprise—he was a lapsed Catholic from New York. He explained that he came from a devoted and large Italian, Irish family and was raised in the church. He then proceeded to ask me questions about the faith.

I told him what I knew, but sadly, it brought to light what I did not know. By the grace of God, I ran to find books to read up on what I did not know. We talked for hours about faith and how to live it. I gave him all the homilies and ideas that had affected my life.

He was an angry man, and I think his heart had been turned off by cultural teachings. I believe this because I was working my faith through the same issues.

I thought he needed a wife. I went every week to a eucharistic devotion sponsored by the Portuguese community, and every time I returned to work I could see the grace of God working in his life.

But I was to learn it was not a wife that he needed. This young man went to confession and started attending Mass. He joined the parish, and we went to a prayer group hosted by Father Thomas Koller, OCD. His own pastor, Father Shea of Holy Family in Glendale, California, took him under his wing

He started to discern his own vocation and found his true spouse speaking to him—God. He was accepted to the seminary, and we kept in contact through e-mail for the next eight years. He finished his seminary education in New York City, and I journeyed to both of his ordinations, one for the diaconate and the other the priestly ordination. He was ordained this year to the priesthood and is now at St. Helena in Bronx, New York.

I learned what a true friend really is: one I could share my most inner and private thoughts with, both negative and positive, and not have to self-censor in fear of what someone might think. When St. Paul talks about unity, I have a vista into what that means now according to faith. Before, it was clouded by our secular culture of over-sexualized individuality and privacy.

If I had not heard all those homilies, if others who shared their faith with me had not spoken up, and if I had not opened my mouth to speak about Our Lord, all this would have been missed.

Wendy M. Posh   *Covina, California*

A Heartfelt Celebration

A distraught mother asked a priest to allow her daughter to receive her first holy Communion without attending a Communion class. The girl, who had a hole in her heart the size of a dime, was scheduled for open-heart surgery, and the mother wanted her to receive Communion before the operation. She said her daughter was well versed in *Catechism of the Catholic Church*, and a discussion with the child proved this to be true.

The priest told the mother that he could not permit the Communion to occur on the upcoming Sunday.

"But I promise next Sunday we will schedule a church celebration," he assured the worried mother.

She concurred, and all announcements were published and read to the congregation so that everyone might come and pray for the child on her first holy Communion and for a safe operation.

The following Sunday, the priest was flabbergasted as the Mary Mother of God Parish Church in Flagtown, New Jersey, filled to capacity. All the aisles and entrances to the sanctuary were packed. The Mass started, and the songs, prayers, and homily were explicit to the occasion.

The startled priest related that in all his days of priesthood, he had never seen nor heard a congregation so engrossed in song and prayer as they were on this day. It was a grand celebration.

On the following Wednesday, the family proceeded to the hospital for the child's surgery.

On Thursday, they returned to the church to give thanks to God. Prior to the operation, a final check was made, and the problematic heart miraculously was healed.

The following Sunday, the congregation gave thanks to God for the gift this child had received.

The priest who celebrated Mass that day was my brother, Father Anthony Martin Kramarz, who was laid to rest on April 30, 1998. An avid follower of St. Anthony of Padua, St. John Vianney, and Pope Pius X, he was appointed pastor of the Mary Mother of God Parish in June 1969, where he served until 1980, when he went to the St. Stanislaus Kostka Church in Sayreville, New Jersey.

Walter P. Kramarz   *Trenton, New Jersey*

A Healing Ministry

In the early 1980s, I was a social worker at Delaware County Memorial Hospital. This is a mid-sized community hospital that sits between two high schools, one of which is Msgr. Bonner High School. At the time, one of the most popular priests teaching at this all-boys school was Father Fitipaldi. Sadly, he had to retire at a young age when he was stricken with Parkinson's disease.

I met Father Fitipaldi around 1982 when he started visiting patients in the hospital on a regular basis. He was very friendly, and the hospital staff enjoyed his company. I always felt sorry for him, though, because I heard a lot about what a wonderful teacher he had been and how much the students loved him. I couldn't help but wonder how he felt having a brilliant mind and not being able to share his gifts with his students anymore.

One day Father Fitipaldi had an exacerbation of his illness and became a patient in the hospital. I went to visit him and shared what I had been thinking. I asked him how he felt coming to the hospital to visit patients now that he was unable to teach. This gentle and kind man took my hand and told me that, while teaching had been wonderful, his ministry at the hospital went far beyond what he had ever dreamed.

He explained that the parish priests who cover the hospital every day only see the patients who have listed their faith as Catholic, or who have requested a visit from them. He, on the other hand, was free to visit with patients as the spirit led him.

Father Fitipaldi said he often stopped in a patient's room at random only to have the patient tell him he had been away from the Church for many years and had been wondering how to come back home. Some patients who weren't Catholic just wanted to talk with him, and they came away with a better understanding of our faith.

Not only did Father Fitipaldi bring many people back into the Church, but he also helped many who were angry and bitter to find peace in their final days. Father Fitipaldi ministered to the sick in this hospital through most of the 1980s, until he became too ill to continue. He remained in residence in a parish rectory until the Lord took him home. I could almost hear the Lord say with a smile, "Well done, my good and faithful servant."

Mary Lou Pappolla   *Bryn Mawr, Pennsylvania*

Hearing the Voice of Jesus

One of my favorite priests is Father Purcell. I first met him on a *Cursillo* weekend about six years ago and learned so much from his inspirational talk.

Father Purcell is the kind of priest everyone loves to have as a friend. He is very personable and friendly, and has a dry sense of humor. He looks very dignified and reverent with his thick, pure-white, well-combed hair and his dark-rimmed glasses. He can look at you with a serious, straight face and then quite suddenly you will hear the funniest genuine comment come out of his mouth. Then you will see his striking blue eyes start to twinkle as his whole face lights up and the entire congregation has a good laugh.

Father Purcell expresses his humility and human frailties quite openly in his humor, despite his many years of service to the priesthood. I remember a Mass when two Protestant men, who were highly motivated to become Catholics, were receiving the sacrament of the holy Eucharist for the first time. Father Purcell humbly admitted in his homily, "When I was asked to instruct these men in the faith, I thought I would be able to teach them a thing or two, but they were well-prepared and they taught me some things about the faith that I never knew."

Although he is retired, Father Purcell claims he works harder now than he ever did when he had his own parish. He celebrates Mass at least weekly at St. Edward's parish in Chillicothe, where I live, and also visits the nursing homes in the area to cheer people up and to bring them Jesus in the holy Eucharist. He always seems to be available to give our pastor time off when he needs it unless he has a prior commitment at another parish. He is in such high demand that he once told me that he said four Masses in one day in different parishes throughout the diocese. He always has a nice word to say to everyone and is consistently very gentle and kind towards others.

Father Purcell is probably one of the most popular confessors around if one can measure popularity by the length of the reconciliation lines. This year at Christmas time, when four other priests were available to hear confessions in our parish, his line was the longest. Every time I go to him to receive the sacrament of reconciliation I close my eyes and feel as if I am hearing the voice of Jesus, as he is so merciful and personable. After he had given me absolution recently, he thanked me in a personal way for my ministry as a lector at daily Mass on Mondays. I was touched not only by his words, but by the way he said it. It brought tears to my eyes.

Father Purcell often smiles and waves at others when he silently processes from the altar to the sacristy. You can't help but smile and wave back at this charming, humble, loving man who gives so much of himself to others and to God.

Jean M. Heimann   *Chillicothe, Illinois*

Feed My Sheep

Father Tom Vandenberg has been our pastor at St. Vincent de Paul in Federal Way, Washington, for twenty-three years.

I was his sacristan from 1985–2000, but when he asked me if I would be his sacristan, I had no idea what the responsibilities would involve. I was eager to learn, though, and he was very patient and taught me what I needed. He sent me to liturgy workshops, which I found to be not only interesting but also challenging. Liturgy has more meaning to me now.

Father Tom is an inspiration to me as I watch him celebrate Mass. When he is at the altar, his heart and soul are in every word he prays. There is an eloquence about him. One day during the consecration these words came to mind: "Feed my sheep." As Father Tom prepared our heavenly meal, I thought this is what Jesus was talking about, this is what he has called Father Tom to do for us—feed His sheep.

To me, all the liturgies Father Tom presides in are very meaningful. I always look forward to Holy Week. The services during the Easter triduum, as he prepares and presides, are so rich in meaning, that after going through the previous days, Holy Saturday is exceptionally joyful. I have never been disappointed.

Father Tom is always ready to help and to listen to any problem I have. He shows such compassion and love during reconciliation that I leave the reconciliation chapel in peace.

Father Tom will be celebrating his forty-third year in the Priesthood in May. He is a gift and a blessing to all of us at St. Vincent de Paul. I thank God that Father Tom answered His call.

Ina E. Ingram   *Federal Way, Washington*

God, Father Bob and Me

I had not gone to church for over thirty years. In fact, I had no real belief in God at all. Then, during advent of 1997, everything changed when I decided to return to God. Although I had gone to Mass a few times in the weeks before Christmas, I had not gone to confession. When I finally went to receive the sacrament the week before Christmas, my confessor was Father Robert (Bob) Naglich, who was assigned to St. Mary's Parish in Crown Point, Indiana.

I worriedly and hesitatingly made my confession by first admitting that I had not been in the church for over thirty years. He answered with a hearty, "Welcome back!" Father Bob's response was heartwarming and unexpected. Instead of a long and possibly painful lecture, he simply and enthusiastically welcomed me back, just like Christ would probably do. But a greater revelation was soon to follow.

Father Bob was patient and understanding throughout my confession. Then, before granting absolution, he said something to me that I had never grasped in all my life. He said to bear in mind that there were three of us in that confessional: God, Father Bob, and me. It was a soul-opening statement he made to me. I had always viewed confession as a dialogue between just a priest and myself. Now I finally realized that it's a dialogue between God and me, with the priest as a go-between. God is actually there longing for the truth and wanting to forgive me.

Something different happened during that confession that had never happened to me before. I walked out of there a changed person. I did not sin like I used to and began to be a *regular* churchgoer. My outlook on many things such as euthanasia, abortion, and other serious matters also changed after that confession.

Father Bob taught me that a priest is a true servant of God and an earthly shepherd for His flock. With his inspirational statement that there are three of us present during confession, he brought me firmly back into the fold of our Catholic faith. I keep that in mind anytime I go to confession.

I would not have returned so fervently to the church had it not been for Father Bob. He brought a soul back to the church, and God said to him on that day, "Well done, good and faithful servant."

Remo J. Tonelli   *Lowell, Indiana*

A Special Anointing

On March 15, 2003, my husband was very close to death. His kidneys had failed, a tube was put down his throat to help him breathe, and his heart stopped. I saw a look of terror on his face and phoned my parish priest. Since I couldn't reach him, I called another priest who was a friend of the family and told him how sick Philip was. Father Jacques Johnson said he would come right away to give Philip the sacrament of the anointing of the sick.

When Father Jacques arrived, he prayed, asking God to take Philip if it was His will. He also told God how grateful he would be if He would heal my husband as a sign of inspiration to all of us.

Forty-eight hours later the doctors told me they were amazed at my husband's progress, and a couple of days after that he was released from the intensive care unit. A week later Father Johnson called to tell me he had gone to see Philip at the hospital. He remarked how my husband was doing so much better and seemed to be back to his old self again. He said, "I never thought you would be taking him home from the hospital." I replied, " I haven't taken him home yet."

My husband was transferred to a rehabilitation hospital and was getting stronger every day. He was due to come home on April 23, but the Lord decided to take him to his true home on April 22. Father Jacques Johnson was with me shortly after my husband's death and made the comment that he really hadn't expected Philip to die. I responded, "Up to one hour ago, I was planning on taking him home tomorrow. We know not the day or the hour when the Lord will come back to take us."

I really believe that the sacrament of the anointing of the sick gave my husband five more weeks of life to enjoy, during which we were able to thank God for His gift of life. Not too long ago, I heard another story of how this sacrament touched the life of someone I know.

One night at RCIA we were discussing stories on healing and I was sharing with Sister Aline, SCIC. She told me about an incident that happened to her in 2003 when she went to the emergency room of the hospital with severe back pain. After having x-rays, she was told that she had a tumor on her kidney that was probably cancerous.

Sister Aline said she was not worried because Father Patrick Baska from St. Alphonsus Parish in Edmonton had given her the sacrament of the anointing of the sick before she had left for the hospital. Two weeks later when she had more x-rays, there was no tumor present.

I recently discovered firsthand how a seemingly simple blessing from a priest can also bring about healing. Earlier this year, on February 18, 2004, I twisted and bruised my leg from a fall, and had difficulty walking. The next morning after Mass, I asked Father Baska to bless my leg because I was in severe pain. After he asked God to bless and protect me, I hobbled away and went to my store.

At around ten o'clock that morning, I remember telling someone about my fall and how sore my leg was. When I went to the post office at four o'clock that afternoon, I realized that the pain was gone. The next morning I told Father Baska about it and he said my healing was because of my faith and the mercy of Jesus. It has been ten months since my injury and although I still have a scar on my leg, the pain has never returned. Thank you, God, for the gift of the priesthood and for holy priests.

Janet P. MacLellan   *Edmonton, Alberta, Canada*

Always a Part of the Family

After being away from home for a few years, I was lucky enough to attend a Mass celebrated by Monsignor McFadden at the Carmelite Monastery in Reno, Nevada, in 2002. After three years, I still remember and can ponder the main idea of the homily he gave. The story of people coming down a mountain after having reached their goal at the top, and encouraging those who were on their way up to continue, was simple but lasting.

Monsignor McFadden's sermons, peppered with humor, have been like this over the years. Jesus' Good News is presented in a joyful way that makes following the right path pleasant and possible, despite difficulties encountered.

Even though he is now Monsignor McFadden he will always be Father Mac to me and to hundreds of others. Father Mac has been a priest for over fifty years, making disciples for Jesus through his writing filled with engaging humor, his welcoming manner, and his wonderful celebration of Masses—some at homes for special occasions.

Father Mac was always welcomed at homes, even when he showed up by surprise (maybe it would make mom run a little), but he was a part of the family. His wonderful sense of humor has always been delightful, and one of his latest newspaper articles in Reno was about what he would do if he became pope for a day. He said, because of his association with the cereal since childhood, that he would make the man who invented corn flakes a saint—St. Will Corn Flakes?

Many are blessed to know Monsignor Leo E. McFadden and experience his faithful following of Christ.

Sr. Janet I. Cavilia   *Fort Lauderdale, Florida*

My Son the Priest

New priest Father Timothy Reid likes to joke that the hound of heaven is no Chihuahua. He found that out firsthand.

Only a week after his conversion to the Catholic Church, Reid said he felt a calling to the priesthood. He resisted it.

"I didn't want to be a priest," Father Reid says. "I told God, 'Listen God, you got me as a Catholic, can you back off?'"

Later, while attending a parish mission, the missionary priest invited those who felt they had a vocation to the priesthood or religious life to come forward for a blessing.

Again, Reid resisted.

"I knew that I should go up to the altar, but I hardened my heart," Father Reid says. "I was more intent on doing my own will than God's will."

The missionary priest persisted. He even personalized this request to the audience.

"You know who you are," he said. "You can feel the pain in your heart. You can come talk to me afterward."

Reid sat at the end of the pew. He eyed the back door. He was poised to make a hasty retreat.

But then the priest processed through the church with the monstrance. As he passed Reid, he stopped.

"You're the one being called to the priesthood," he said.

"Yes, Father, I know," Reid said, sighing.

That night Reid prayed that if it were God's will for him to enter the priesthood, his heart would have to be changed.

"I woke up the next morning with a big smile," Reid says. "I could only think, 'I want to be a priest.'"

There is no shortage of vocations.

But there is a shortage of young men willing to say Yes to their call. How can we help our own children break down the barriers to that Yes?

Here are a few pieces of advice from the experts—priests.

1. Let Them Meet Priests

Bishop Michael Burbidge, a Philadelphia auxiliary, is crystal-clear about what inspired his own vocation to the priesthood—other priests.

"It was really through the priest presence in my Catholic high school that I was encouraged to examine the priesthood," says Bishop Burbidge, former rector of St. Charles Seminary in Philadelphia, where twenty-two dioceses send their seminarians. "There were eleven priests teaching at my high school and I saw them as a group. There was something special about them."

When Burbidge mentioned what he was thinking to his young parish priest, the pastor helped him to discern his vocation.

A similar approach has led to tremendous success in the Diocese of Bismark, North Dakota. There, in a diocese with thirty-eight active priests, exactly half that number are currently in seminary formation. The majority, according to diocese vocations director Father Thomas Richter, have come from the diocese's three Catholic high schools, all of which have active priests teaching in them.

"How does a young person get to know a priest above and beyond weekly Mass?" Father Thomas Richter asks. "Many young people don't even get to know a priest through youth groups anymore."

Finding ways that young men can meet holy priests is one of the strongest ways for parents to encourage priestly vocations.

An active outdoorsman, Father Gregory Mastey, vocations director with the diocese of St. Cloud, Minnesota, frequently goes trapping, fishing, canoeing, and hunting with young men and their fathers from his own parish, Mary of the Immaculate Conception in Rockville, Minnesota. He encourages parents to invite priests to their homes and their children's sporting events.

"Every priest can point to other priests who have had an influence in their lives," Father Mastey says. "Have priests over for dinner, invite them to go with you to an athletic event, learn about the priest and his interests."

Jason Asselin, a twenty-eight-year-old seminarian, is in his third year of theology at St. John Vianney Theological Seminary in Denver, studying for the Diocese of Fargo, North Dakota. Asselin says his vocation was encouraged by his grandmother and then, after college, through priests.

"I met several young priests who were very dedicated to their vocation," Asselin says. "Each of them loved being a priest."

2. Be a Generous Family

Pope John Paul II also has a recommendation about vocations. He says that "families are the seedbed of vocations."

"The best method of fostering vocations within families is for husbands and wives, fathers and mothers to live their own vocation generously," says Father Tom Wilson, vocations director for the Archdiocese of St. Paul and Minneapolis.

"All vocational calls are about living a life of generous service and fidelity," he says. "When kids see in their parents that Christ comes first and serving others takes precedence, they are much more likely to respond 'Yes' if God is calling them to a life of generous service within the church."

Father Richter conducted an informal survey regarding the family size of seminarians.

"On average, the family size for many brothers, sisters, and seminarians was about five children," Father Richter says. "While there are exceptions to the rule, married people who generously live their vocation tend to form kids who want to generously live a God-centered life."

Father C. John McCloskey, ordained in 1981 for the personal prelature of Opus Dei, agrees. He grew up as the oldest boy in a family of eight.

"Growing up in a large family showed the fruitfulness of generosity in self-gift," he says. "That played an important role for me."

"If you were to do a survey, you would find a disproportionate number of priests are the oldest boy in the family," he adds.

3. Help Them Discover Prayer

Father Reid recommends prayer and fasting for vocations—for parents and for interested young men.

"Vocations don't grow on trees," he says. "They need to be cultivated over time with our prayers and penance. I know a lot of people who fast weekly for vocations. It works. I believe in the depths of my heart that I am a product of that."

"A family that is going to promote vocations to the priesthood has to be eucharistic," Father Richter says.

"When all is said and done, a priest exists for the Eucharist."

Father Peter Williams, parochial vicar at St. Vincent de Paul Catholic Church in Brooklyn Park, Minnesota, agrees. One of nine children, the Eucharist was central to both his priestly vocation as well as the vocation of his brother, Father Joseph Williams.

"Nearly every day from kindergarten through twelfth grade, my father took us to daily Mass," Father Peter Williams says. "That is where my vocation was born, in serving and being close to the Mass…in praying and staying close to the sacrament of reconciliation. The mystery unfolded before our eyes."

Father Brian Herlocker's vocation came through spiritual reading as a U.S. merchant marine. Originally from the state of Washington, Herlocker's father was a Quaker; his mother was Lutheran.

"I had a lot of time to think about things on the ship and lot of time between girlfriends," Father Herlocker says.

While aboard an oil tanker in Alaska, he saw a copy of St. Augustine's Confessions lying around. It was a shock to Herlocker, who was more used to seeing pornography left out on ship.

"I read it and it turned my world upside down," Father Herlocker says.

"It made me stop and think about what I was doing with my life."

Father Herlocker now serves as a priest in the Diocese of Peoria, Illinois, where he works with college students at the University of Illinois at Urbana-Champaign's Newman Foundation.

"I tell incoming seminarians that their home has been the first seminary," says Father John Allen, vocations director for the Diocese of Charlotte, North Carolina. "It is there that the life of prayer and piety, the life of joy and service, is first developed. It is the work of seminary formation to build upon that foundation of the family."

Father Richter adds that children need to see the ways in which the priesthood enriches their parents' lives.

"It's in how the parents speak about the priesthood and in talking with the children about the homily after Mass," Father Richter says. "It's in supporting the parish priest when he is trying to promote programs."

In the end, perhaps there are as many ways to foster priestly vocations as there are vocations themselves. One thing is for certain—the Holy Spirit provides.

Tim Drake   *Saint Joseph, Minnesota*

This article originally appeared in *Faith and Family Magazine* and is used with the author's permission.

Tim Drake is the author of *Young and Catholic: The Face of Tomorrow's Church* (Sophia Institute Press, 2004). He writes from Saint Joseph, Minnesota.

Building a Happy Family

Father Gilbert was a Franciscan priest from a nearby monastery who helped at our parish on weekends. One Sunday (I believe it was the Feast of the Holy Family), he preached an inspiring sermon about bringing families closer together. He encouraged us to build happy, holy families by loving and forgiving those with whom we live, and to do delightful little things for them. Then, as he ended, Father Gilbert said, "To make a home, always remember—'Happiness of Others before Me!'" The words of this holy priest made a lasting impression on me as a teenager.

Elizabeth G. O'Connell   *Catonsville, Maryland*

Part of God's Healing Plan

I have a deep, abiding faith in God that surprises some people because of my personal experiences. God is my intimate friend, my strength, my stronghold, and my safety in the midst of life's traumas.

My childhood was colored by repeated abuse, and because I was so young, it became my *default program* to accept it and say nothing. My choices as an adult continued to reflect that early *programming* until I began working with a gifted and resourceful therapist, Goldye Donner. By then I had been abused emotionally, physically, and sexually at home, at work, and at church.

In the midst of this darkness, I found an oasis of peace in the daily quiet time I spent with God. The deeply painful, depressing memories were balanced by the strength I found in God and the safety I experienced in therapy. With God's help and Goldye's support, could I weave those positive experiences into the negative threads of the garment that is me, creating a new tapestry?

At about the same time that I was recovering from memories of my sexual abuse, the church began confronting her own history of sexual abuse. In fact, I believe that the church is prophetic in her actions dealing with the scandal. By identifying, admitting, and publicly apologizing for behavior that also occurs in families and in society, I am hopeful that the church is setting an example that society and families will follow.

But what about this victim of sexual abuse? What about my own healing and resolution? It is a long and difficult journey. God, in His great wisdom and faithful provision for me, sent a new pastor to All Saints Parish while I was in the throes of discovery in therapy. Father Bob Cilinski is everything I could want or need in a pastor. He is kind, caring, respectful, affirming, encouraging, humble, attentive, and appreciative.

146

He is part of God's healing process for me, demonstrating by words and behavior that he is trustworthy. I meet with him from time to time.

In the fall of last year, he was asked by our bishop to say a Mass for healing for victims of abuse. Coincidentally (or not), I met with him a few weeks before the Mass to share some of my writing and to receive his counsel. He told me about the service on October 21 and asked if I would allow him to share some of my writing with those who attended. I was honored, humbled, and delighted to say "Yes".

When the evening came I was in the sanctuary feeling vulnerable and scared. It would be the first time I had been in a public setting that addressed the abuse. It would be the first time anyone had read my writing in public. It would be the first time I had received acknowledgment of God's gift of writing to me.

The Mass was more than I could have imagined or hoped. In his homily, Father Bob looked at the experience of the Israelites enduring the abuse of slavery and then the difficult journey through the wilderness before reaching the "promised" land of milk and honey. He compared it to our journey following the abuse, to reach a place of healing and hope.

Father Bob's prayer for victims of abuse in the period following his talk was moving and powerful. He said, "I pray that God will open your eyes to see your own goodness. I pray that God will open your ears to hear the positive and compassionate words people speak to you. I pray that God will open your hearts to receive healing and allow you to trust again."

Beautiful, spare words of prayer gently placed in pools of silence. I let the prayer soak into my soul. At a level beyond words, I knew that healing had begun.

Later, in my journal, I wrote, "I never expected to feel so positive. I feel all 'sparkly' inside, kinda like I'm carbonated. Instead of Kool-Aid, I'm full of fizz. It's a good feeling."

Janet L. Smith   *Gainesville, Virginia*

Pearls of Wisdom

Jesus never said, "Pick up your light cross and follow me." He said, "Pick up your cross and follow me." This is just one of the pearls of wisdom I have been blessed to receive from my spiritual director, Father Bill Ashbaugh from St. Joseph Parish in Howell, Michigan. Not only does Father Bill say deeply meaningful phrases that I can remember when life is challenging but he has been a big part in my freedom from a gambling addiction.

On March 15, 1997, which happened to be my birthday, I purchased a lottery ticket at a Meijer store. Then, almost a year later, as I was traveling to Westphalia, Michigan, to hear a speaker at Father Bill's parish, I heard over the radio that a lottery ticket worth $34 million dollars had not been claimed. If the winner did not give the ticket to the gaming commission by March 16, 1998, he would lose the money. I just knew that the ticket was mine.

Although I spent weeks searching my house, van, and office, the ticket never surfaced. Some people tried to get me to use psychics, which is against our religion, and each day a new idea popped into someone's head as to how I could try to find the ticket.

Finally I found a stack of lottery tickets, and two weeks of them were missing—the week of the winner, and the week prior to that. I learned that two weeks before the radio announcement my mom had burned some old lottery tickets, and I realized that the winning ticket must have been one of them. I kept praying to St. Anthony for assistance but had a sinking feeling that it truly had been burned. I was soon to become the biggest loser in the state of Michigan. During this difficult time, Father Bill counseled me on the phone almost daily.

St. Patrick's Day arrived and it was now official—the search for the $34 million dollar ticket could stop. I remember sitting in the pew after Mass with tears streaming down my face. I had big plans for that money with various charities, but it was not meant to be. I went to my office and called Father Bill. He said to me, "That ticket was not found because it would not bring you any closer to heaven." He made it sound so simple, which is one of Father Bill's many gifts. He can always make tough situations seem easy.

After the lottery ticket incident was over, I had this strange notion that God wanted me to have money. I began gambling heavily at the casino and with the lottery. To complicate the matter, as a Catholic youth minister, I did not have money to spend gambling.

I went regularly to confession and the penance was always one that would help me break the habit. The first penance was no gambling for all of Lent. I tried to protest because my friends usually took me to the casino for my birthday which was during Lent. Thankfully, Father Bill would not budge.

The next penance was really tough. I had to donate the amount of money I wasted at the casino, which was $500, to charities. That amount was a fortune for a church employee. It took me six months to decide which worthy charities to share my money with.

Despite this, my gambling was still out of control and I knew it. My last penance was the hardest—no more casinos, period. That was the one that finally liberated me from gambling. I gave up the casino November 24, 1999, and have slipped only once since then. That time I was nudged to go and believed I could enter a casino and not gamble if I didn't have money with me. I was wrong. My sister gave me money when she won, and I found myself back in the confessional and completely staying away from casinos after that. I gave up the lottery on November 12, 1998, and when the lottery jackpots are high, I pray I am not tempted.

In his book, *Introduction to the Devout Life*, St. Francis de Sales discusses the value of a spiritual guide. He says, "He will be a treasure of wisdom for us in our difficulties, our disappointments, and our failings. He will be a remedy and comfort in our spiritual illnesses. He will not only protect us from evil, but will assist us at our spiritual betterment and growth."

For me, this quote describes Father Bill. We met in 1993 as chaperones for World Youth Day in Denver. I was lost for hours with four others and he found us. Since that time he has been keeping me on the right path, whether during a pilgrimage to Italy and Bosnia, while on EWTN's *Life on the Rock*, through discussing how to overcome gambling, or to merely deal with everyday life issues.

The Diocese of Lansing is blessed to have Father Bill as a priest, and I am so very fortunate to have him as my spiritual director. He has helped me grow closer to Our Lord, the Blessed Mother, the saints, and even my guardian angel. Thank you Padre Bill!

Lisa A. Stechschulte   *Howell, Michigan*

The Unknown Priest

Every country has a memorial to the *unknown soldier*. This story is my memorial to all the *unknown priests*. Those are the priests who, with a word, a challenge, or a smile, effect a radical change in our way of loving and perceiving God. One such priest was a Franciscan friar who gave a weekend retreat for married women several years ago.

I had deliberately taken some over-due time out from my hectic life as a mother of five children and a wife of a busy politician. I was so eager for some spiritual refreshment that I didn't even care who the priest would be. I only knew I needed a couple nights of solitude and quiet, with time to reflect on my spiritual life that was often neglected due to my exhaustion.

Once at the convent, we were assigned to our rooms and then directed to the dining room for a light supper. We were informed that this was a *silent* retreat, so meals were eaten with no conversation. What a change from Friday night supper at home!

After supper, we moved into the warmth of the tiny chapel, waiting expectantly for our first session and meditation. As I sat there, I was so overcome by the lack of pressure and the quiet that I barely heard what the priest was talking about. But then, all of a sudden, I perked up as if God had nudged me to stay alert for what was coming next.

I looked at the priest (whose name to this day I cannot remember) standing in his simple dark brown robe and sandals. He spoke in soft but deliberate tones to the women assembled. "So you see, that is why we must never imagine that when we do something wrong God will remove Himself from us, even if we have hurt Him, or if He is displeased or even angry. Put a picture in your mind of you and God standing face to face looking at each other. If you do something wrong, something sinful, it is not God who backs away from you. It is you who backs away from God. You are creating the distance between the two of you. He has never moved. He is still standing in the same place, remaining constant, desiring you to ask forgiveness and step forward to be face to face in union with Him again."

As I listened, I felt a total shake up inside myself. I realized that my entire life had been wrongly based on the idea that God withdrew Himself from me when I sinned. It had never occurred to me that I was the one who had the choice, that I was the one who created the distance, not my ever-loving Creator. He was always there for me. Just like the father of the prodigal son.

The words of this dear Franciscan at that retreat created a profound change in my view of my relationship to God. I can never thank God enough for allowing this *unknown priest* to be His instrument of insight for me at that memorable retreat. I returned home on Sunday afternoon with a deepened understanding of God's unconditional love, and a determination to try to imitate it with my husband and children. Dear *unknown priest*, wherever you are now, thank you for those words that changed my life.

Lorraine M. Williams   *Markham, Ontario, Canada*

You Must Take Christ With You

Fifty years is a long time to wait to join the church, but that's what I did. The year I joined was the same year our new priest, Father Jack, came to our parish. During the RCIA classes he was very helpful; no question was too small. We also had fun because he has a great sense of humor. He has been an inspiration to me ever since.

At one point I went through a really tough time. He told me that if I ever faced a difficult time like that again to come to him right away and he would help me through it. It is a great comfort knowing that he will be there when I need him to counsel me.

Father Jack radiates Christ. In everything he does, you can see that Christ is at the center of his life. He says that if you leave Christ in the church, you are wasting your time going to Mass. You must take Christ with you when you leave, and live your faith.

With so many priests being talked about in a bad light these days, I wanted to share the good news about this devoted priest who lives his life for the Lord. There are many, many dedicated priests like him all over the world that we never hear about because they don't make the news. What a shame.

I have been ill for four months now and unable to attend Mass. Father Jack visits me faithfully every month. He is not a young man. In fact, he came out of retirement to take this parish. Sometimes it is hard for him to walk up our steps, but he does. When I receive the Eucharist and give my confession, it is such a blessing. I am very fortunate to have a priest like him in my life.

Lynn C. Couser   *Punxsutawney, Pennsylvania*

My Guardian Angel

In June of 2002 my husband suffered a serious fall and was in the hospital for nearly a month. During this time and throughout the remaining months of Nel's life, our dear friend Father Keith, who lives just a mile from us here in Cincinnati, Ohio, was my guardian angel.

My husband had suffered from dementia for a number of years, so anything that caused change was very difficult for him. It was only through Father Keith's kindness and steady help, including his help in locating a very reliable nurse aide, that I was able to keep my husband home in familiar surroundings.

For nearly four months Father Keith came to my home most mornings to help me get Nelson up and dressed for the day, and he returned in the evening to help me put him to bed. Regardless of how stressed Nel was during the day, in the evening he eagerly awaited this special priest's visit.

Father Keith would greet Nelson with, "Hi, Captain! How are you doing tonight?" A big smile could be seen on Nelson's face when he heard those words. His father had been a sea-going pilot, so any reference to that brought a great deal of happiness to him.

This kindness, plus having someone really sitting down and taking the time to converse with him on his level, quickly calmed my husband down after a long day. With Father Keith's help, I was then able to get him cleaned up and ready for a restful night, which he, and I as the caregiver, needed.

Father Keith was there to help me in caring for my husband, and was a strength that I could lean upon. Any caregiver will tell you how important it is to have someone in your corner for support. Caring for a spouse with dementia and severe physical problems can be extremely taxing, both physically and mentally.

Regardless of how unpleasant or icky the problem at hand, Father Keith was someone I could always turn to and depend upon. On more than one occasion, he left his tasks, even if he was in the midst of preparing a meal, and came to pick Nel up off the floor or help me move him so I could clean up an unexpected accident that my husband had.

I will be forever grateful for the kindness shown by this caring priest during our time of need. Even in his poor state of health, my husband saw Father Keith's compassion. A few nights before he died he asked this wonderful priest to take care of me. I know my husband is looking out for me from heaven, but it is most comforting to know that I don't have to face my problems alone. I have a concerned priest who is a friend always ready to help.

LaVern I. West   *Cincinnati, Ohio*

My First Communion Party

I was born in Pittsburgh, Pennsylvania, in 1969. As a child, I attended Carlow College Catholic School during the week and went to Saint John Fischer's for Mass on Sunday. Father Cicola was our parish priest, and he was wonderful!

At my first Communion party, my mom asked me to come in from outside because someone was here to see me. There in my family room was Father Cicola! He had actually come to my first Communion party! I felt so special that day, and that feeling and the memories of him have stayed with me throughout my life.

This past August I attended a Christ Renews His Parish (CRHP) retreat at St. Jude's Catholic Church in Allen, Texas, where my family and I now reside. After my retreat, I began thinking of Father Cicola extensively. During adoration one Tuesday, I kept getting the feeling that I should give him a call and let him know how much he has meant to me all these years.

It took exactly two calls to locate him. I made the second call while driving. The woman on the other end said, "I am sorry to tell you this, but Father Cicola passed away a few months ago." He died March 4, 2004, at the age of sixty-three. Needless to say, tears streamed down my face when I heard the news. I was crushed and thought, "Now he'll never know how much I love him."

The angel on the phone told me how to get in contact with Father Cicola's brother, and I called him a couple of weeks later. Although our grief was still fresh, we had a beautiful conversation and were both happy I called. I am assured that Father Cicola knows how much I love him and how much of a positive impact he had on my life. I pray to him and tell him that frequently.

Gina Marie Schafer   *Richardson, Texas*

The One Who Sent Jesus

I first met Father Donal O'Mahony on October 7, 1978, at the feast of the Holy Rosary. He belonged to the White Fathers of Ireland and had been in Nigeria for twenty-three years when the Biafran War broke out. He and his fellow missionaries were given an hour to leave the country. He had only the clothes he was wearing and his breviary. Some of the people in his parish took his chalice and buried it because the authorities would not allow him to take it.

His plan was to return as soon as the war ended. In the meantime, there was no hope of his returning since his sponsoring bishop had died.

156

He settled down at St. Catherine of Siena Church in Metairie, Louisiana, where he endeared himself to all, especially the children and the elderly in poor health.

One of his fellow priests who had been stationed with him in Nigeria told us the following: *Father O*, as he was affectionately called, had a parish of seven thousand and went into the fields to celebrate Mass with and for them. It took over an hour for him to give the Eucharist to his parishioners. But he did it willingly and joyfully!

There was an elderly man who lived in the *bush* whom he had catechized and later baptized. Father O told him that he would bring him the Eucharist on a given Sunday. Before Sunday could arrive, one of the man's relatives came running to Father O to say that his uncle was dying and wanted to receive the Eucharist as soon as possible. Father O got into his Jeep and traveled in it as far as he could go, then went the rest of the way on foot.

When he arrived, the man was already dead, but his relatives began to tell Father O that another priest had come to give their uncle the Eucharist. Father O knew that there was no other priest for hundreds of miles around, and, therefore, this could not have happened.

When Father O asked the relatives to describe the priest's appearance, they explained that the other priest wore a white cassock just like his, and that he carried the Eucharist in a little pouch just like his. In describing his facial features, Father O realized the description matched that of a picture he had given the elderly man at his baptism. All the villagers swore that *a priest* had come to bring the Eucharist to this elderly man.

Father O's conclusion, as well as that of everyone else, is that Jesus Himself was the *priest* who answered the fervent plea of the dying man and sent an angel to bring him the Eucharist. This word spread through the villages in Nigeria, and Father O became known as the "one who sent Jesus" to their dying relative.

I had the privilege of taking care of Father O when he became ill with Parkinson's disease. He died in 1995. His funeral Mass was celebrated in a packed church that held one thousand people with standing room only. He is sorely missed!

Sr. RoseMary Wessel, MSC   *Metairie, Louisiana*

Living the Love of God

As a child I had little to do with priests. Our parish seemed to have very old ones who rarely touched on subjects of interest to small minds. When I was a teenager, a gifted young priest was sent to us for a few years, and he touched the lives of numerous young people. At college in Georgetown I met a few more priests, yet I tended to stay clear of them, not really understanding who they were or what they were all about.

When I moved to San Diego in 1999 I was quite startled when the pastor of my new parish walked up to me after Mass and introduced himself. It was my first time at St. Brigid's, which is a large and dynamic parish in the youth-oriented beach community of Pacific Beach in San Diego. I found a panorama of programs for all ages and interests in that parish, and was especially drawn to the small group communities, the faith and prayer groups, and the Little Rock Scripture programs. Through these activities I got to know the religious sisters who ran these programs, and enjoyed their lively wit, big hearts, and deep faith.

Over the course of four years, I began to realize that what really held the parish together—from a committed staff to interesting, faith-filled speakers, to lively community events, to top-rate music and packed young adult Masses—was the depth of faith and commitment of our pastor, Father Peter.

As it always seems to be the case, it is when we are in trouble that we discover our true friends. Well, trouble must be my middle name because I'm knee deep in it more often than not, and I don't bear suffering as quietly and mildly as one ought. So, I made a lot of fuss and bother as I went through some difficult spiritual struggles during those years.

Looking back, I can see how Father Peter struggled to direct me spiritually, and how he tried to help me embrace peace and the other fruits of the Holy Spirit. However, mine was a difficult spiritual adolescence. He was pretty special and strong in faith, hope, and love to put up with me for as long as he did.

One night it all seemed to come to a head. I went to a community penance service and found myself faced with a disquieting sense that, as I stood on the brink of a proverbial cliff, my latest ravings to God had gotten me into big trouble. In some ways I saw myself for the first time. Somehow, through that priest, I recognized my own sinfulness. I felt I had pained someone who had consistently and generously given of himself for the benefit of his sheep. That really hurt.

That night some of my negative behaviors and attitudes began to change. I credit Father Peter for helping me turn away from unhealthy attitudes and assumptions and begin to be truly open to the heart of our faith and the love it calls us to. I knew the forgiveness and mercy of God when I received absolution that night.

That, I know now, is what priests are all about. They are called to live the love of God in their own lives and parishes, and to have a willingness to be God's instrument in the human stories that play out all around them.

I have known many good teachers in my life, have had good friends, and know the love of family. Yet there are few people I have met who are willing to go beyond ordinary expectations and desires and to be open to the transforming power of God's love. I thank God for sending Father Peter into my life, even if it was only for a brief time.

May God bless all the priests, deacons, religious, and lay faithful, and open them to the great gifts bestowed on them. Help them to be a transforming presence in their families and communities. And may our young hear your call, Lord, and fill the vocations needed in our churches and religious houses today.

Sharon E. Reidy   *Cottonwood, Arizona*

Double Blessings

I am a cradle Catholic who strayed away from the church for nearly thirty years. I grew up in Lansing, Michigan, where I attended The Church of the Resurrection. In the Jubilee year 2000 I found myself being drawn back to the Church. This is when the Lord blessed me with Father Jeffrey Robideau, the parish priest at Resurrection.

Father Robideau was very encouraging and patient with all my questions. I felt as though I needed to relearn many issues that I had forgotten and learn the changes that had taken place in the Church in the last thirty years. Soon this very special priest had a great part in making my sisters and brother also feel comfortable in returning to the Church.

He took my brother-in-law, a non-religious man, under his wing. Working like a guardian angel, he helped him through baptism and confirmation. Not just one, but nearly an entire family returned to—or found—the Church.

Father Robideau introduced my sister, brother-in-law, and me to the Discalced Carmelite Secular Order. There he taught us how to deepen our faith in prayer and, most importantly, helped me with my vocation.

God also blessed me with wonderful neighbors: devout Catholics. Their son, Patrick Hawkins, was home on summer break from the seminary in St. Paul, Minnesota, and I asked Patrick to help me with learning the Liturgy of the Hours. Since I was a new aspirant to the Discalced Carmelite Secular Order, I felt intimidated with the prayer book because it was difficult for me to understand and follow.

Since Patrick prayed the Liturgy of the Hours throughout the day at the seminary, he understood the prayer book quite well. As he patiently worked with me, I was touched by his love for this prayer and felt eager to learn all I could. I saw a glow in his eyes, and I wanted to sense what

160

he was illuminating. Soon I realized that this beautiful glow came from within. It was his deep love for God and for speaking his word.

Soon I will give my first vow, and as I go through my vocation I will thank Patrick for his inspiration and for the imprint he left on my heart. I thank God for leading Patrick through his vocation for he will certainly be a blessing to the priesthood. I also thank Him for the gift He gave to Father Robideau: the gift of speaking the truth. I thank the Lord for bringing him into our lives. I know we have been blessed with a grace from above for both Patrick and for Father Robideau.

Debi Jean A. Hill   *Lansing, Michigan*

A Roman Catholic Priest in Today's World

In the fall of 1998 I was at work in a local flower shop. Father Bill Hritsko, associate pastor at St. Francis de Sales Church in Newark, Ohio, walked in the door. I thought he looked familiar but wasn't positive because he was not in clerical garb. He introduced himself after I offered to help him, and the rest is history.

We both grew up in very ethnic families in northeastern Ohio. Both of us still had aging mothers living in that area. Father Bill visited the flower shop several times and, after our conversations after Mass and at our Social Hour, I invited him to dinner in my home.

We talked for a very long time about our families, our experiences growing up in an ethnic environment, and how we both came to be in Newark. We also had a deep conversation about our faith that awakened in me a prayerful life that had been put in a closet.

During the first year I knew Father Bill I was going through some very difficult emotional situations. My deep-rooted prayer life, instilled in me by a grandmother who had lived with us at home all my life, had become too casual. I was experiencing problems: a long friendship had come to a bitter end, my children and grandchildren lived out of state, and I had some health issues. To top everything off, no legal action had ever taken place with my husband of twenty-four years who had moved out of our home twelve years earlier.

With the guidance, prayer, support, care and concern of Father Bill, I was able to put my life back on track.

Both of us are night owls so Father Bill and I began working in the church with the flowers and plants in the evenings. It wasn't long before people started observing the flowers and mentioning how much they liked the warmth and beauty they brought to the church.

From day one Father Bill became a member of our family. Holidays and special events were complete only when he arrived. Even the grandchildren asked if he would be at a holiday event.

Over the four years that Father Bill was at St. Francis, he helped me through a very long, drawn-out and messy divorce; he helped my son and daughter-in-law prepare for their sacramental marriage, the baptism of my son's six-year-old stepdaughter, and later, that of his infant son.

Father Bill has a sixth sense about peoples' needs. It is not uncommon for him to just show up or call at times when you really need some guidance or someone to talk with. "Something bothering you today?" or "Do you need someone to talk to today?" he will ask. He will listen as long as you need to talk and then "ask" if you want his opinion or advice.

His homilies are outstanding, spoken to you, not at you. He encourages us to practice our faith openly, to share it with others, to look deep within ourselves for ways to expand our practice and to make good use of the sacraments. He frequently draws in some of his personal experiences as a professional dancer and his theater performances to relate his lesson to us. For those paying attention, there is something in every one of his homilies that address your own personal needs, shortcomings or gifts.

His reverence during the celebration of Mass is absolutely impeccable.

Father Bill is a multi-talented person who shares his many talents with everyone. During Father Bill's four years in Newark he participated in several shows in our community theater, including portraying Captain

Von Trapp in the *Sound of Music* to thirteen sold-out audiences. He has an outstanding voice and plays just about every string instrument there is. Among his many other talents he also designs and sews his own vestments. Frequently, he is called upon to design and make chasubles for other priests. He has even made our bishop a chasuble and miter.

For me personally, through his gentle encouragement, I have once again gotten involved in church activities, becoming a Rite of Christian Initiation of Adults catechist and sponsor and a special eucharistic minister. I am also involved in the children's liturgy and much more.

Three years ago Father Bill was transferred to another parish not far from Newark, but he left a wonderful mark on our entire church community that will not be forgotten.

My friendship and work with Father Bill continues. He remains an integral part of my family and the many other families whose lives he has touched at both St. Francis and at his current assignment.

Father Bill Hritsko is, like all humans, not perfect. But his dedication to his priesthood, his insight into people's needs, his willingness to help people regardless of their faith, his vision and his artistry enhances the church and Mass celebrations, and his devotion to our faith and his priesthood makes him a shining example of what it is to be a Roman Catholic Priest in today's world.

Rose Marie Maddern   *Newark, Ohio*

My Faith Was Challenged

After I joined the Community of the Monks of Adoration in 2002, I really thought my life had found its fullness and I was on a clear road straight to the will of God.

"What could prevent me now from doing everything God wanted me to do?" I thought. I was very happy to face anything for the sake of Christ in the Eucharist (which is our community's charism).

But then *anything* visited and my faith was challenged. I began to get sick. No one knew why. Many doctors agreed to see me on a charity care basis. Our local Catholic Hospital of Bon Secours also extended an enormous amount of charity care on my behalf. So many tests were being ordered that we could never have afforded it otherwise. Even our local county health department became a much-needed resource, because, in spite of the many medical minds working on my case, no one could tell me what was going wrong in my body.

Soon I was bedridden. The best the physicians could do was to tell me to go to bed, rest, and try to "ignore the pain." I obeyed, and month after month I remained in bed. A year went by, and the only times I got out of bed were to go to yet another doctor's appointment, or to a hospital ward for another procedure and examination.

Then it became very clear I needed *the* physician! It was suggested by my superior that I might want to consider receiving the anointing of the sick. Since we are a newly formed community with no resident clergy, we rely on the local priests of several parishes for our sacramental needs. I thought I should pray about which priest to call, and I was led to ask Father Rafael Padilla of Our Lady of Lourdes Parish in Venice, Florida, to give me the anointing of the sick.

Since traveling even short distances was extremely painful, Father Padilla came to my cell in the monastery. We prayed together, and he anointed me with holy oils blessed especially for the purpose of anointing the sick. Afterwards, we sat in silence for a few moments, and then he began to speak.

"You know, Brother Mark," he began, "sometimes Jesus does not heal us all at once, but slowly and over time. And sometimes our physical health is not what returns to us, but we are given a greater spiritual health for having received this anointing."

He seemed to speak very quietly and deliberately, as if to be sure I was taking in what he was trying to tell me, and of course at that moment, I thought I understood. But as months passed and my physical pain continued, and at times got worse, I realized I didn't understand him at all! But I continued to pray that God's will be done in me. I had been reading about the lives of many blesseds and saints, mostly of modern times, and how they suffered a wide variety of bodily ills, some of them never being healed but actually succumbing to their diseases.

Soon I began to see what Father Padilla so wisely told me. It was taking time for me to get well and free from most of the pain. In the meantime, however, my soul was realizing that I was being accompanied along the way by the priest of our salvation—Jesus Christ Himself. And the night Father Padilla came to anoint me, he wasn't coming alone at all! It was Jesus Christ, the great physician Himself, who was inviting me to take hold of the hem of His garment as Father anointed the various parts of my body. It was the presence of Christ in that priest who was calling me forward into a life of greater faith by *not* healing me instantly, as He could have, but rather healing me very slowly, step by step, as each day I accepted His invitation to "launch out into the deep" with my nets and not allow myself to feel defeated and think of my bed as my final resting place.

Father anointed me in June of 2004. Early November was the first time I saw Father again. At the Mass he was celebrating, I stood before him to receive Christ again in the Eucharist, our eyes met. He smiled broadly, as did I. It dawned on me then how this priest so wisely planted a seed of faith in my heart, by telling me the truth that my road may still have a few bumps in it, but to trust in the will of Christ. And there at the altar, as we smiled at one another, he again delivered Christ to me and invited me to live a more faith-filled and sanctified life. This time I was standing up by the mercies of God. I was not lying flat on my back!

I never asked Father Padilla what he was thinking at that moment he saw me, but I hope that he somehow knew that my smile betrayed my joyful thoughts: that he was right all along in what he told me, and that I was more than blessed to know Christ more, through him in his presence in my life.

Br. Mark E. DeBrizzi   *Venice, Florida*

A Warm and Welcoming Church

The year was 1991 and I was beginning a new life in a new state. At the time I was an oncology nurse at St. Thomas Hospital, and as I began my search for a church home, some of my co-workers told me about St. Edward's Parish. I will never forget the first Sunday that my mom and I went to Mass at that warm and welcoming church.

When we arrived for Mass, people were chatting on the sidewalks and said "Good morning" to us as we walked by. Father Joe Pat Breen was at the door greeting people, and from the way he acknowledged us, you would have thought we were his oldest and dearest friends. He even invited us to stand up and introduce ourselves to everyone before the Mass started. Not only did he remember our names, but he remembered the names of other visitors as well. The next Sunday we went back to St. Edward's and Father Joe Pat still remembered our names and where we had moved. Wow!

Back then there were 900 families in the parish and Father Joe Pat was the only priest. Now there are over 1,500 families, and he is assisted by other priests. Complain and grumble about the awesome workload? Not Father Joe Pat: He gets his congregation involved in doing their *thing for the Lord*. Many people who thought there was nothing they could contribute to the parish found out what God wanted from them with Father Joe Pat's help. He doesn't tell them what to do—he gently leads them to find their niche.

I know that if he reads this, this humble priest will try to pass the praise to others. Many people feel the same way I do about Father Joe Pat Breen. He demonstrates what the priesthood is all about, and we are proud to call him Father. Praise be to the Lord!

Rosemary J. Hanley   *Springfield, Missouri*

My Conversion

I was raised in a Catholic family and practiced our faith throughout my adult life, but my true conversion didn't begin until 1990 when my husband and I were about to retire.

At the time we had a big decision to make. We owned two homes—one in Edmonton, Alberta, Canada, and the other a lovely cottage at Mann Lake in North Central Alberta. Since we couldn't afford to keep both places, we decided to sell the home in Edmonton and move to the lake. Looking back, it was the most important choice I have ever made.

As we settled into our new surroundings, we learned that the little church we had attended on weekends at the lake had closed because of a lack of priests. We now lived in the diocese of St. Paul, Alberta, so I called the cathedral and spoke with Father Edmond Croteau, who had been the priest at the church that closed. He suggested that we go to Sacred Heart Parish in Vilna, a little town about fifteen miles from our home. That's where it all began.

In 1993 Father Edmond was appointed parish priest at Sacred Heart Church. The next year, when the diocese began a lay ministries program, he gave me a brochure about the program and told me to fill out the application and send it in. As I skimmed through the information, I said to myself, "I'm too old to begin that." But Father Ed would not let me be.

The next Sunday after Mass he asked me if I had sent the application in yet. When I said "no," he encouraged me once again to send it in. Then on Monday he called from St. Paul to say he wanted to stop and see me on his way home. By the time our visit was over, the form was completed. I realized that Father Ed had pursued me for a reason and thought, "Wow! God must really want me in this program."

The program was called Emmaus Lay Ministries Program, and it changed my life. It was a three-year program where the group studied

Scripture, Church history, liturgy, prayer, and the understanding of ourselves. We spent one weekend a month for ten months at a diocesan retreat facility sharing what we learned and forming a community relationship. It was an awakening in my life that I am so thankful for. Our class graduated in 1996.

I have since become active in my parish, and was also professed as a secular Franciscan on October 4, 1996. Thank you, Lord, for Father Edmond Croteau, who was the instigator of my conversion.

Pauline T. Saretsky   *Ashmont, Alberta, Canada*

A Special Priest

Father William Karath was a special priest whose life was one of incredible adventure and inspiration. He was filled with awesome talent and had a big influence on the lives of others. Born February 21, 1946, he lived on this earth for only fifty-six years, and yet all those who knew him have been changed forever.

For thirteen years, Father Bill was our best friend at St. John's Mission in Port Orford, Oregon. He shared our joys, trials, and pain. He helped our community endure the sorrow of suicides and murders of many young people and a few older people. He brought comfort to us as we mourned the death of a young man, assuring us at the funeral that Jesus would be very sad that the boy killed himself, but that He would take the boy into His loving arms. Another time, an entire family with two young children was murdered. Even though this was extremely painful for him, he continued to counsel and comfort the people in our community as well as those in surrounding areas.

His sermons were off the cuff and kept us at the edge of our pews. He encouraged us not to be reluctant to help others, and we went home from Mass confident that we could make a difference in the world. He taught us that we are all sinners, including him, and that we just needed to do the best we could. We learned from him that when we fail, God will forgive us, no matter what we have done.

Father Bill had a lighter side to his personality, and his sense of humor was wonderful. After Mass, he always told jokes, and on St. Patrick's Day, he would wear shamrocks on his head. At Easter time, he wore bunny ears as he led the children in the Easter egg hunt. Children of all ages loved Father Bill. He loved teasing the older kids, and for many years, he taught soccer at Catholic Central High School in Portland, Oregon. He was an excellent teacher who was known for instilling good sportsmanship in the students.

During the time he was with us at St. John's Mission, Father Bill baptized so many Hispanic babies that we almost lost track of them. Once he almost baptized the same baby twice! He didn't speak Spanish very well, but all of our families loved him. People would come from as far as twenty-five to fifty miles away to go to his Masses because he always made them feel part of our parish family.

Father Bill was not in good health because of the malaria he had contracted in Africa when he was a young missionary. Also, he had been a very active athlete—a runner and a soccer player—before an injury crushed one of his feet. These health problems were difficult but they never stopped him from being a wonderful priest.

Father Bill died on January 11, 2003. He had been ordained in Rome on December 17, 1971 and touched many lives as a priest. The archbishop and about eleven priests and ministers of other faiths came to his funeral. The Mass was a large celebration of his life, and afterwards there was a dinner with lots of laughter as we shared stories of his life.

I know I speak for many others when I fondly remember this funny, compassionate, and loving priest. We miss Father Bill very much, and always will, but I feel that he is still influencing our lives, guiding us to be the best we can be.

Joyce A. Iida   *Sixes, Oregon*

New As A Baby

Father Louis D. Berube was a priest of the old school. He was devoted to his mother and, even in his old age, still became teary when he spoke of her, particularly when repeating the story of how the neighbors had gathered around to recite the rosary as he was being born.

This man knew hardship all of his life—losing family members at young ages and then leaving his loving family in Massachusetts to go to seminary in Montreal, Canada. He was a priest for nearly sixty-five years.

During his priesthood Father Lou was an educator, scholar, and rector of our cathedral which caught fire and burned to the ground in 1949 under his watch. It was said that he went into the burning church to retrieve the Blessed Sacrament from the tabernacle, getting our just before it was totally engulfed. He went on to build one of the most beautiful cathedrals anywhere. It now stands as a monument to Mary, Jesus and Father Lou.

When he was in his early nineties he had become frail but still continued to say daily Mass at his residence. He also walked about a mile to the hospital to visit the sick each day and continued his visits until two months before he died. In fact, Father Lou walked everywhere, and in so doing became a visual picture of our church: a priest, visible to all. I might add that he was also a friend to all, no matter their faith, always stopping to chat and always a "God bless you" upon departure.

I was privileged to have him as my confessor until near the end. I would sit in a little wooden chair across from him as he sat in his reclining chair. I can see his face today as I look back, for when he was there, his entire face changed and his prayerful self came through. He was no longer a jovial man, but was a serious, different man. He had become my Jesus before me.

On one occasion, I prepared myself for the sacrament of penance by writing all I could think of that I had done to offend God. When I began my long litany, my confessor listened carefully.

After I finished, Father Lou stood up, came over to me, put his feeble arm around me and held my head. He said, "You have prepared very hard for this, and I want you to forget it all, for when I give this absolution, it is gone, never to be remembered. You will be as new as a new baby coming into this world."

With those words, he laid both hands upon my head and gave me absolution.

I had never felt so free of my sinful affliction in my life. Father Lou really taught me the value of the sacrament of penance—how totally forgotten our past will be. I could have done cartwheels out the door and down the street.

I was a neighbor to him and became a close friend, caring for him in every way with the help of many other faithful friends. I was with Father Lou the day he passed. He was in a great deal of pain but never uttered a complaint. When I had to move his pain-ridden body, he only sighed.

Just as he came into the world, Father Lou passed into eternal life with the rosary being said all around his bed and with the love of his devoted friends who cared for him. The voices became louder and louder as he slipped away on the lilt of Mary's prayer. I can still hear those voices.

Father Lou, Monsignor Louis D. Berube, PA, left this world on September 17, 1999. I am a better man for having known him, and he forever changed my way of thinking of the sacrament of penance. I can now walk free. I miss you Father Lou.

Stephen L. Henry   *Ogdensburg, New York*

A Promise to the Priesthood

I was always told that the call of the priesthood sometimes begins in the heart of the mother. My story begins like that.

I was brought up in the Catholic faith and went to Catholic grammar school. My sister and I used to sing every Sunday in the folk Mass, which paved my way for my teenage years. The priests at Holy Cross Church in Brooklyn, New York, were always very respectful and like second fathers to us. We had no other social life as pre-teens and teenagers, as my father was a very strict Italian man.

As I lived in fear of my fathers' severe, stern ways, I would turn to the church for guidance and support. I did not have the kind of relationship a daughter sometimes has with her father, being *daddy's little girl*. My father loved us deeply, but he was not the type to communicate with us or to verbally express his love. Our mother surely made up for that—God bless her. That's how it was back then.

It was inevitable that I would turn to the priests and nuns for the guidance and emotional support I so much needed. Sharing and assisting in those Sunday Masses and listening to the Gospels and sermons from Father Joseph Morales and Father Richard Bory meant a lot to me. It was my only consolation that kept me strong and on the right path.

Finally, in 1996, as an adult, when I became confused and needed to know the purpose of God's mission for me, it was the priests that God placed before me who kept me on that right path: Father Fussner at St. Peter's Church on Barclay Street, Wall Street, New York, and, most especially, the missionary priest, Father Sebastian, who, with the intercession of St. Therese of Lisieux, prayed with such untiring fervor for her *shower of roses* to be given to me before he returned to his native homeland in Banglore, India. These two priests tremendously assisted me personally with such grace and patience that it is nearly beyond comprehension.

I am deeply indebted for their love, prayers, and support given to me during that time of trial and tribulation that I endured. They will forever be in my prayers. It didn't matter whether they were young, middle-aged or old. Their persistence in helping me never grew tired or cold.

I am eternally grateful to Mary's priests for their hard work, sacrifice and prayers that often go unnoticed and unappreciated in today's world. I am also grateful for the priests who assisted me throughout my lifetime in Mass, holy Communion, confession, and all the sacraments. I will continue to keep them in my prayers every day because I know I have been truly blessed to have met all those priests who made such an enormous difference in my life, not only in the delicate years growing up which are so vitally important, but also in the most recent years as an adult.

Almost seven years ago God blessed me and placed before me a wonderful husband. Just a year before meeting him I received the calling in my heart for our son to enter the Priesthood. I made a promise to our Blessed Mother that if I am blessed with the state of motherhood, I will hold myself to that promise and be very proud and, I hope, worthy, to be the *mother of a priestly son.*

Nita A. Cybruch   *Staten Island, New York*

Passover Seder—A Family Affair

I'd like to present Father Ashley Harrington, the pastor of Immaculate Conception Parish in Norwood, New Jersey. He is a very humble, wonderful priest who helped create a beautiful Passover Seder tradition in our church.

Somewhere around 1987, Father Ashley went to great lengths to learn the Hebrew prayers and to speak the language correctly. He got most of his information from my husband, who is Jewish, and through various books. The parishioners responded very positively to this affair, which we named, "Passover Seder—A Family Affair."

By our third Seder we had a couple of hundred people attending, which was amazing. Everyone participated in organizing it, and that was quite a feat. It was great to see such enthusiasm. We tried to make it as accurate as possible, and of course, we had Father Ashley portray Jesus.

It was very heartwarming to see us learn about our Jewish roots and to experience more of how Jesus actually lived on this earth. If it weren't for Father Ashley's complete love for this project it would not have been successful.

Ruthann P. Weinstein   *Cape Coral, Florida*

My Own Missal

When I was a little girl in the late 1950s, my family was poor. However, since everyone in the working class neighborhood I grew up in was the same as us, we didn't really consider ourselves lacking. We had enough food to eat and a good home but no money for any *extras*. Our family life revolved around home, church, and school.

I attended Our Lady of Perpetual Help parochial school, and our parish church was across the street from it. One day when I was eight years old, I was walking back to school with a friend after lunch when she asked me if I wanted to go to the rectory of the church with her so she could buy her own missal. I agreed to go because I knew we had enough time to stop and not be late for school.

The housekeeper opened the door and asked us what we wanted. My friend told her she wanted to buy a missal, and the lady told us to follow her. She led us into a room that was much like an office.

A minute or so later, Father Blanchfield walked in the room. He was a big man, about six feet tall with broad shoulders. When he asked us what we wanted, my friend told him that she wanted to buy a missal. As he reached into his desk to retrieve one, he said to me, "What about you? Don't you want one too?" I said, "Oh no, Father Blanchfield. I don't have the money." Missals cost $1.50 at the time, which was a lot of money for us. My friend paid Father Blanchfield, and then off we went to school.

Around two o'clock that afternoon, there was a knock at our classroom door. My teacher answered it, and it was the principal, Sister St. Terrance. She whispered something to our teacher, and then called my name. She told me to come to see her during recess. I was frantic, wondering what had I done to deserve a call to the principal's office. By recess time I was in a panic mode. My hands were sweating as I made my way to her office.

When I knocked on her door, Sister St. Terrance told me to come in. Then she picked something off her desk and handed it to me. It was a missal! She said, "Father Blanchfield sent this over for you." I was ecstatic! I had my very own missal! I kept thanking her over and over again, and she said, "Don't thank me, thank Father Blanchfield."

That's exactly what I did after school that day. Although I was a very shy little girl, I went to the rectory and thanked Father Blanchfield at least twice for the gift he gave me. He smiled and chuckled as he said, "That's all right." I quickly left to go home and was so excited I felt like I was walking on air.

I'm now in my 50s and have never forgotten that act of kindness from Father Blanchfield. When I was little girl, he touched my heart, making an everlasting difference in my life. I grew up with a respect for and a soft place in my heart for our dear priests. When the abuse scandals came out and people were deriding all priests and bishops, I warmly remembered how special and kind Father Blanchfield was.

This thoughtful priest has since passed on, God rest his soul. Although there was only one Father Blanchfield, I know there are many more like him out there, quietly doing their work and making a difference in people's lives. Those humble priests never receive recognition; they never hit the front page of a newspaper. Thank you Father Blanchfield!

Sandy E. Whalen   *Kingston, Ontario, Canada*

Let Go and Let God

In our parish, the most Holy Name of Jesus-Blessed Kateri Tekak-witha, Father John Hascall has taught us that the Eucharist is the greatest medicine God has given the people.

When Father John celebrates Mass he seems to have a special connection with God. On one occasion our son was very sick with convulsions, and I was overcome with fright. I went to Mass where Father John was the celebrant, and I experienced a miracle during the consecration. As he raised the host, the words he spoke opened my heart to hear Jesus speak personally to me of His love for me and the importance of my relationship with Him. When we discussed the *whisper* that I heard during Mass, Father John said, "That must have been the Spirit talking, not me. I don't talk like that, that's the Spirit."

That Mass changed my life. Father John's faith and belief in Jesus' presence in the Eucharist opened a new life in Christ for me. Because Father John's relationship with Christ is so evident, my faith increased and I was able to hear Christ whisper in my heart. Father John is dedicated to the Gospel and to living it as Jesus said his followers would do. He calls his people to fast, pray, and sacrifice to make them stronger.

He teaches that in the Eucharist God is timeless and Jesus is always present and that when he celebrates the Eucharist, healing occurs because Jesus is there with us. People have come from all over the continent to be present at a Mass that Father John celebrates. Through his kind and gentle spirit, however, he always makes sure that the people know that it is God who does the healing, telling us: "At every Mass, healing should occur because we come into the presence of Christ's passion, death and resurrection."

And truly, the Spirit heals through Father John. At Christmas 2004, all of our sons were home for the first time in five years. At Mass, Father John reminded them, and everyone, of God's healing love and forgiveness. Within a few weeks after that celebration, one of our sons was facing a very difficult medical problem. I was praying that my son would hear God's voice and God's direction. Father John talked to me on the phone and reminded me to let go and leave it all to God's will. He promised me he would pray. Father John prayed, I slept, and my son received God's direction in the wee hours of that morning. Although he did not know that I had asked Father John to pray, my son told me, "I felt God's hand."

Father John comes to the people as a simple man speaking truth, accepting us with all our faults and mistakes. When he addresses a mistake or fault, it is with love, and it is in a way we are able to move forward and not dwell in fear and the difficulties of the past. He speaks out against injustices that cause people's suffering, and teaches through his actions the way to live life with a respect for all.

Father John is respectful of the cultures of different people, using the languages and traditions of the people he is among, in just the manner that the Catholic Catechism states that the liturgy be celebrated. When he does this, the hearts of the people are softened and Jesus is recognized. When he says Mass in the language of the Ojibwa, he breaks down barriers for the indigenous people so that they might know Christ. His special gift for the Native American people allows him to reach out to those who have experienced so much suffering and been subjected to countless iniquities.

When I was filled with worry for my son, he told me to put a flower in my room and to ponder, each day, how God makes that flower grow. In this way, Father John taught me how to "let go and let God." It was the hardest thing I ever learned—and I am still learning. I say "*Miigwitch*" (Ojibwa for thank you from the heart) to the Creator for blessing the people with priests like Father John.

Cynthia A. Bertagnoli   *L'Anse, Michigan*

The Parish Is the Body of Christ

I was in my thirties when I returned to the Catholic Church in 1987, and Father John Deitzen was the pastor of the huge historical downtown church that I chose as my new parish. I don't recall our first meeting, but I shall always remember his kind and friendly manner, his warm, welcoming smile, and his twinkling eyes and rosy cheeks.

I left the Catholic faith following a painful divorce, and now, after seventeen years, I had returned to my faith as a single, professional woman, looking for something more than the secular world had to offer, looking for something to fill the void in my life.

I was working as a school psychologist at the time, and Father Deitzen's intellectually stimulating homilies filled my mind with new ideas and practical examples that I was able to apply to my everyday life. His words nourished me but left me wanting to know more about the mysteries of my newfound faith.

After Mass he always stood in front of the church on the sidewalk at the bottom of the concrete steps and greeted everyone with a smile, a handshake, and words of good cheer. He was always ready with a positive comment for everyone he greeted. Young and old gathered around him, engaging him in conversation, as he was quite charismatic, and his good nature, his natural interest in others, and genuine humility drew people to him.

His homilies and his spiritual guidance inspired his entire congregation to become involved in various ministries. For example, when one couple began attending early morning Mass together, he asked if they would like to serve as eucharistic ministers. They replied that they would both like to serve, but the wife stated that she was not Catholic. Within a short time she began taking instructions in the faith, and they became

178

eucharistic ministers and leaders of various ministries within the church. The husband later became a deacon in the parish.

One of the groups this couple led was Renew, which brought parishioners together in their homes to discuss topics of their faith on a weekly basic and to take individual or group actions based on their discussion. It was through participation in this group that I grew in my faith and became determined not to just be a *Sunday* Catholic but to live out my faith in my life.

During the first few years as a member of this parish I became more and more involved in my faith, attending daily Mass and holy Communion. I participated in Renew groups and became a Renew leader and facilitator. I attended Adult Enrichment classes, joined the prayer group, and became a member of the choir. However, I still felt a yearning to do more—to express my gratitude to God for welcoming me, His prodigal daughter, back into such a loving and faithful community. And it was Father Deitzen, the pastor who resembled Jesus in so many ways, who made the parish "the body of Christ."

I later learned that the church I choose to be my new parish had a very active evangelization group in which the active couple, now my new friends, were participants. This group had been praying fervently for a return of Catholics to their faith, as had the entire parish. There was so much love in this parish. It started at the top with Christ and channeled its way down the ladder. The moderator for this group was Father Deitzen, and as I grew in my faith, both he and the couple invited me to give my witness to the group. Other fallen away Catholics told me that my witness touched them deeply, and they expressed interest in returning to the Church.

Even though I had come a long way, I continued to cling to my worldly ways. I desperately desired to remarry and have children before my biological time clock went off, so I began to pray fervently for a husband. Soon I began dating an attractive, intelligent, college-educated young man with whom I had a lot in common. We became engaged to be married, and we started the annulment process under the direction of Father Deitzen.

I knew it would take a long time due to the complications involved— ours were not *simple* cases. However, I remember angrily approaching

Father Deitzen once and interrupting him in the parish center toward the end of one the evangelization group meetings, complaining that I was sick and tired of waiting so long. It had been over a year and nothing was happening, and he needed to do something.

Calmly, Father Deitzen tried to explain to me the reason for the wait and scheduled an appointment for me to meet with him. Everyone in the group was kind and empathetic and treated me in such a loving manner, despite my outburst. Instantly, I felt the love and peace of that group reaching out to me, although I was still ruffled.

Time heals all things, because the waiting made me realize that the one thing that mattered the most in my life—my faith—was missing from the relationship. It was not until after I made a *Cursillo* weekend (a weekend retreat for Christians) that I began to realize that something was amiss. I began to question the practicality of marrying someone who seemed to be growing further and further away from me as I was growing closer to God and stronger in my faith.

Although he had been raised as a Christian, my fiancé admitted that he was actually an agnostic and when I began to play Christian music he became angry and insisted that I immediately turn it off. When I invited him to Mass, he angrily refused, and he expressed strong criticism of the Catholic Church. When I began to open my eyes to the truth, I discovered there were other serious differences that would prevent us from having a successful marriage. I believe that it was Father Deitzen's prayers and assistance that prevented me from making a tragic mistake.

God gave me the courage to finally break off the relationship. My fiancé accepted my decision but was not happy with it.

A few months later, I learned through a friend who worked at one of the local hospitals that he was in the Intensive Care Unit and had nearly died. During his hospital stay, it was Father John Deitzen—a Catholic priest—who went to visit the man who strongly hated the Catholic Church and was a self-proclaimed agnostic. I don't know what happened during that visit, but I do know that my ex-fiancé lived and recuperated, even though he had experienced a stroke-like condition that paralyzed the entire right side of his body, resulting in permanent brain damage and memory loss. He was without family, so I continued to visit and assist him for a couple of years afterwards as he made the transition from the emergency room to long-term care and independent supervised living as he regained some of his skills.

I knew that God answered prayers, and He eventually brought an attractive, intelligent, college-educated faith-filled Catholic man into my life. It was Father Deitzen who met with us for our marriage preparation courses. It was Father Deitzen who, after meeting my husband-to-be for the first time, winked at me as he led us to the door and whispered, "I think you found a good one this time." I can't recall if he added, "You'd better hang onto him," but it was definitely implied. We have been married now for nearly thirteen years.

Father Deitzen is a retired priest in the Peoria, Illinois Diocese. He remains active in his priestly duties, although he no longer serves as a pastor of a parish.

Jean M. Heimann   *Chillicothe, Illinois*

A Friar with the Eyes of Jesus

It was the Depression era, and my father was born into an immigrant family living in downtown Chicago. They were parishioners of the famous Franciscan parish, the old St. Peter's at Polk and State Streets.

Among the friars in that house was the famous Franciscan, Father Pat. My father used to tell me how the kids just flocked to him because of his deep concern for their welfare and his profound holiness. Papa related that Father Pat always had an open-door policy, and it was a common event to just drop-in on him.

On one occasion, when Papa went over to see this awesome friar, an event transpired that changed my father's future forever, as well as the lives of future generations.

"Hi, Father Pat!" my father said, greeting the gracious friar.

"Hi, Dominic, me boy. What brings you here?" Father Pat asked, to which my father replied that my grandmother had made some pasta fagioli and homemade bread for him and the other friars.

"Oh, Dominic, your mama cooks like an angel from heaven," Father Pat said. "Thank you so very much. I am sure that the friars will enjoy this tonight. Now tell me, my boy, how is school going?"

My father said that school was just fine and that he was nearing graduation from high school at De La Salle. Father Pat then inquired as to where he would be going to college.

"College?" my father asked in amazement. "Oh Father Pat, my family could never afford to send me to college."

With that comeback, Father Pat's Irish eyes twinkled. "Just a minute, Dominic," he said.

Father Pat went over to the phone and dialed.

"Hi, Joe, this is Father Pat," he grinned into the phone. "What time is that race today? Really? Well, I will be sending this kid over, and he is a great runner."

Father Pat hung up the phone, turned to my father, and told him to immediately go to Grand Crossing Park on the Southside of Chicago. He was to compete in a race for a full scholarship to De Paul University.

My father started to argue a little, saying he did not even own track shoes or the proper running clothes.

"Don't worry," Father Pat said firmly. "Nothing is impossible with God. Now hurry, before you miss the race."

The story unfolds that Papa indeed took the streetcar over to Grand Crossing Park and ran in his street shoes. Not only did Papa win the race, but he also ended up attending school with the original Mayor Daley.

It was because of this holy friar who had the eyes of Jesus to see not a skinny immigrant kid, just four feet and ten inches tall, but rather a giant of a man who would succeed in life because someone believed in him and taught him "nothing is impossible with God."

Thank you Father Pat. I hope to meet you in heaven someday and give you a big hug for you have touched many generations because you believed in my papa.

Mary Lou Schuster   *Joliet, Illinois*

I Always Know I Am Loved

It was the spring of 1983. I was nineteen years old and was soon to be a May bride. Father Roger Caplis, my pastor, was preparing my future husband and me for the wonderful sacrament of matrimony, when one day in early in April, my fiancé told me that he no longer wished to be married. At first I thought, "How strange, is this April Fool's day? Okay, where is the punch line?"

When it finally sunk in that this was no joke, I was devastated. Parties were cancelled, gifts were returned, and we counted our losses. If that wasn't bad enough, my fiancé and I ripped each other up verbally by telling everyone each other's bad habits, errors, deep dark secrets, and anything else we could think of to point that finger of blame. I was utterly ashamed of some things I had done in the past that were now made public; things my parents had not been aware of until then. I lost my mother's respect, and it took almost a year to gain it back.

I called Father Caplis in tears to tell him the wedding was off, and asked to speak with him in person. In a tear-filled meeting, I confessed all of my now exposed sins. He gave me total absolution and a heart-felt lecture about why I needed to set higher standards for myself. Then he saw me to the door and embraced me as he assured me that I was loved, and more importantly, that I needed to love and respect myself. He said I deserved that.

Father Caplis made me feel very special. He went above and beyond the call of duty, and although I have made many mistakes and misjudgments since then, I have never felt alone. I always know I am loved. The last things he said to me that day have helped me stay centered through much turmoil in my life. I will hold onto his words always.

Jennifer L. Garrity   *Chicago, Illinois*

A Living Example—Pope John Paul II

Pope John Paul II was a living example of poverty, chastity, humility, obedience, and charity throughout his life. His was a life of adventure and sacrifice, and he loved the Bible and all of God's creation with his entire being. He often used the pen to teach us about the Eucharist and the rosary and established both the Year of the Rosary and the Year of the Eucharist.

Our beloved pope frequently went to confession, and celebrated the seven sacraments often. He loved our Blessed Mother and said Masses at many Marian shrines including Guadalupe, Chestawova, Knock, Lourdes, Fatima, and Nazareth, among others. He brought new meditations to the rosary called the Mysteries of Light, and he consecrated the world many times to the Immaculate Heart of Mary.

Pope John Paul II did all of the spiritual and corporal works of mercy as our pontiff. He helped the poor in soup kitchens, did missionary work, provided support for nuns, fought for the right to life of the unborn, and reached out to our youth. He was responsible for the new *Catechism of the Catholic Church*, the Nova Volgata Bible, and for canonizing many saints and ordaining new cardinals.

Thank God for the pope's jubilee work, his commitment to always implementing Vatican Council II correctly, his perseverance in the face of persecution, and his reparation for our sins. He never stopped bringing the peace of Christ to the world.

Pope John Paul II had magnificent quotes, such as, "Praying the rosary is gazing at the face of Jesus," and "Keep your eyes always fixed on the Sacred Heart of Jesus who is always our savior." His motto, *Totus Tuus,* and his total adherence to the truths of the Trinity and the Incarnation have most likely inspired many vocations. The Polish phrase *Jezu ufiam tobie!* (Jesus I trust in you!) shows Pope John Paul II's love for the Church's Lord. *Deo Gratias!*

Louis B. Remlin   *Westport, Connecticut*

My Best Friend

At age eleven I began serving at Father John Milanese's Masses at SS. Donatian and Rogatian Church in Randolph, Vermont. Since that time, my life has been changing. From the start, I loved serving for Father John, and I still do. He is always patient when anyone *messes up*. In fact, he is so nice about it that no one wants to ever make a mistake again!

All of his servers look up to him and respect his opinion. Father John is always open and ready to answer any questions. He always pays attention to you and knows when you're feeling down. And he knows just how to cheer you up.

Because of Father John's influence, we now go to daily Mass every time Father has it. He always makes sure all of the kids can understand his homilies, as well as the grownups.

Also, because of Father's interest and encouragement in our home school education, I am taking a classics course in high school. He taught me to aim high, saying: "If you believe in the incredible, you can do the impossible."

Ever since I met him, I have *adopted* Father John as a role model, and I have always considered him my best friend. I am now thirteen years old, and I hope that he will be my confirmation sponsor when I am confirmed in 2007. He is undoubtedly one of the best people in my life.

Johanna Mahaffy, age 13   *East Randolph, Vermont*

He Blessed the Creek

Over the years following Vatican II, for the usual assortment of reasons our family slipped away from the Church. The years took us through a collection of disasters that erased our jobs and transplanted us into an entirely new life. Not until our son's near fatal accident in 1976 did we stop to survey our condition.

On the fifth day in which our son lay in coma, I phoned our new parish to ask a priest to come and bless our new home. My husband had labored for four years to turn raw land into a thriving little family farm, and I was stunned that I hadn't thought to have our home blessed sooner.

It was midsummer. Without a pastor, our parish, St. Mary's in Corvallis, Oregon, was making do with newly ordained priests, fresh from the seminary. The young man who answered our call was excited and joyful to be performing this priestly task for the first time.

His clerical garb was so new it dazzled my eyes. His blessing book was so new that some of its pages had yet to be cut. I followed him around with a letter opener in my hand and often cut the pages for him.

Taking a vial of holy water from his shirt pocket, he started in the kitchen. "The center of every loving home," he remarked, grinning. He blessed every room in the house, sprinkling holy water as he spoke the blessings, even opening closet doors and blessing their contents.

Then he said, "Let's go outside." First, he blessed the well. Ah, yes, pure, healing, living water. Then, riffling the pages of his blessing book, he said, "Do you have any chickens?" I shook my head, no. "Pigs?" Again, no. "Cattle?" Yes. We went to the pasture. He blessed the pasture, and he blessed the calves grazing there.

Then he asked, "Do you have a creek?" I nodded. "Take me to the creek."

We wandered down the shady, cool corridor of the path through the alder and ash trees, past the blackberry brambles, down to the riffles where the trout and crawdads gathered.

"Is this water pure?" he asked. "Yes," I replied, "the Department of Environmental Quality has seen to that." He nodded.

He blessed the creek, dedicating it to God's glory.

Then, leaving me breathless with astonishment, he emptied his vial of holy water into the creek and, stooping to the surface of the riffle, refilled the vial with blessed creek water, stood up, capped his vial, and returned it to his shirt pocket.

Miracles of healing, miracles that transformed the protocols of treatment for head-injured patients around the world flowed from that time and place. Our son, paralyzed from his neck down, came to live with us and left four years later, no longer paralyzed, to continue his healing odyssey.

That young priest, whose name I've long forgotten, put all the joy of his new priesthood into those blessings. And neither he nor I will ever know how far those blessings reached.

Carol Bergener   *Westport, Washington*

In My Time of Sorrow

My wife Rose died on November 29, 2003. The emphysema caused her to suffer greatly for a year and required her to be on oxygen all the time. She died three days after our forty-third wedding anniversary.

The evening after she died, I was at home feeling devastated, terribly lonesome and depressed. At this time, I received a phone call from Bishop Donald Kettler, who was the bishop in Fairbanks, Alaska. He was formerly our pastor in my home parish, and I was his deacon for seven years before his new appointment as bishop.

That evening he talked to me for half an hour. I cannot say how much he lifted my spirits. He was very understanding and helped me immensely in my time of grief and sorrow. I could never thank him enough—a great bishop and servant of God.

Deacon Ralph C. Counter   *Sioux Falls, South Dakota*

Our Biggest Sinners

At our parish Advent service, Father Tom asked that a collection be taken for the poor. He jokingly said that if someone was a big sinner he or she probably wouldn't contribute as much as the more saintly in our group.

Once the collection had been taken, and just before the final blessing, Father Jim, who was assisting at the service, hissed to Father Tom that neither one of them kicked into the collection, thus labeling them as the biggest "sinners" of all!

Both priests grinned, and Father Tom told everyone gathered what Father Jim had just said to him. The people roared. In fact, I've never heard so much laughter at a penance service before or since.

Both priests immediately remedied the situation and probably between them gave a more generous donation than the average person in the pew.

It's refreshing to find that priests can poke fun at themselves and share a hearty laugh with everyone. I'm sure all those gathered were laughing all the way home.

Gloria J. Huerta   *Wheaton, Illinois*

Sitting with Jesus

During the 9/11 crisis I was back home in New York City visiting and caring for a relative who was dying from breast cancer. I had grown up in the area and attended the Catholic grammar school.

During this time it seemed that all the headlines in the newspapers were about priests in the surrounding parishes who had been accused of molestation crimes. I feared that soon the name of the priest who had abused me would be published and it would not be my secret any more. Could I live with myself for not speaking up all those years ago, and what would my family say?

Praise God, my parish was not among the scarred ones. I did, however, need to unburden my soul, but the last person I wanted to reveal this to would be a priest.

When I came back home to St. Edward's Parish in Stafford Springs, Connecticut, I saw my humble and holy parish priest, Friar Richard-Jacob Forcie, anointing a man for a serious illness. He was so caring and gentle and seemed to peer into the man's very soul. I believe at that moment the Holy Spirit picked me up by the shoulders and dropped me in front of the very person who could help me and set me free.

I spoke with him and revealed all that had happened to me those many years ago, and it was as though I was sitting with Jesus Himself. He forgave me for the guilt that I had always carried with my biggest fear: that perhaps my own silence may have led to others being harmed.

From that night when I spoke with Friar Richard-Jacob I have never suffered another horrific nightmare of being hurt. This man has become a very good and caring friend and never makes me feel as if he recalls what I had shared, by the grace of God. I have since become a parish council member and work with the Protecting God's Children Program.

Larraine C. Kennedy   *Stafford Springs, Connecticut*

A Little Lamb

I became an altar server and have served at Mass every day since the first week of June 2004. Our parish is very large, with over 19,000 people. The pastor of our church, Father Andrew Kemberling, personally trained me, as well as Father Mel Thompson, Father Martin Whealen, and Father John Paul Leyba, until I was good enough to serve alone.

Our priests have also helped me along the way with encouraging words. Father Mel and Father John Paul would crack a joke. Father Andrew and Father Whealen would tell me that I'd do fine. At the end of Mass, they'd always make it a point to tell me that I did a good job, no matter how much of a hurry they were in. I know that I'm safe around them because once a man was making me feel uncomfortable and Father Andrew made sure that it stopped.

I can now serve at the alter without any help and, thanks to our parish priests, I am co-training new altar servers with my mother, as well as bringing communion to the elderly and sick every Tuesday and helping her set up for Mass as co-sacristan. I am so thankful to be home-schooled and to be able to be in the Lord's house all of the time.

I am very thankful to have such caring priests who took the time to train me and give me encouraging words that make me feel good about serving. I couldn't be where I am today without them.

Emily L. Westover, age 12   *Centennial, Colorado*

Twice Blessed

In 1999, I attended Chicago's annual Marian Conference. While I was there I went to receive the sacrament of reconciliation. Father Benedict Groeschel was a speaker that weekend and was also hearing confessions.

For some time I had thought that my civil marriage was not recognized by the Church. Our church's new pastor, Reverend Daniel McCarthy, had made mention to the parishioners about seeing him in regard to matters, but I had begun to get involved in the church ministries and was a bit shy about going to see the new pastor about this. Although I knew it was silly, I waited to see a priest I was not familiar with to discuss this in confession.

Father Groeschel was kind and very thorough with me. He did not give me absolution, but he did give me direction. He was so kind and helpful that I felt unburdened and accepted. He took his time and listened to every word I said and explained everything to me. The whole time I never felt judged.

My husband and I did exactly as he instructed us to do. We immediately saw our pastor and took the steps needed to have our marriage blessed by the Church.

I sent Father Groeschel the picture of our ceremony with our sincere appreciation. It was both a blessing and a treasure to have both of our children participate in the liturgy. Our daughter, Veronica, served at the altar, and our son, Ryan, presented the rings to be blessed.

Last year Father Groeschel was critically injured when he was struck by an automobile. He was in grave condition, and I prayed for his recovery. He is now back working and touring, praise God.

But my most wonderful experience with Father Groeschel was that he told me on the day of my confession that I was the answer to his prayers. He shared with me that he prayed to be able to really help someone that weekend, and he felt he did help me. I was, after all, blessed twice with Fathers McCarthy's and Groeschel's care and guidance.

Jennifer L. Garrity   *Chicago, Illinois*

Pilgrimage: A Tribute

As Father Bertrand Conway, a famous Paulist writer and lecturer, tells us, a true pilgrimage must focus on the needs of the human heart and not on satisfying our worldly pleasures. For several years my wife and I were blessed with having a dear priest, Father Joe Kelly, as our guide on our own spiritual pilgrimage through life.

When we lived in the Philadelphia area our children attended parochial schools and we went to the associated churches. After we moved to a town in the Midwest the children attended public schools and in time went off to various colleges. We were parishioners at a local church, but as my wife Louise says, the experience was not spiritually uplifting. I, too, found our religious community static. We had no sense of being on a pilgrimage. That was when a friend suggested we try the Newman Center, where Father Joe Kelly was the chaplain.

During our first visit, Louise recalls being attracted to a poster in the entrance area that read, "There are no strangers here, only friends we have yet to meet." She saw it as a sign for a new beginning. We liked the colorful liturgies, the origami cranes over the altar, the meaningful homilies, the singing, the dancing, and the strong sense of community, although it took us a little while to reach the hugging stage. The openness, naturalness, spontaneity, sincerity, commitment, and gusto of the community created an ambience that impressed me.

Father Joe inspired the community to support each other's personal pilgrimages and to express its collective spirit through the liturgical experience. He also urged us to reflect on the Gospel message in the light of the great need for justice and peace in the world.

We had a two-year absence from the Newman Center while serving in the U.S. Peace Corps in the Fiji Islands. In many ways our Newman experience prepared us for what we encountered in our parish in Fiji. The parish was divided into sectors, and members met in homes regularly. We had a short religious ritual and some socializing, and then planned for parts of the Sunday liturgy when it would be our turn. We cleaned the church, filled the huge seashells with holy water, gathered flowers for the altar (no need to go to a florist), and selected the songs. On Sunday we led the singing and did the readings. This involvement brought us closer to one another and to the pastor.

We have also traveled quite a bit, and each time we departed, we left instructions in our *For the Children* folder. One item read, "In case anything happens to us, contact Father Joseph Kelly, Chaplain of the Newman Center." He had promised that he would say our funeral Mass. At one time Father Joe said, "You will probably outlive me." His prophecy was to come true.

Over the years we have been to many churches, cathedrals and basilicas, and a number of major Catholic pilgrimage shrines. Yet our pilgrimage always brought us back to the humble Newman Center.

I know why I felt so close to Father Joe, and why I came to love him. Like me, he was a pilgrim. Never dogmatically sermonizing, he revealed himself as a sensitive human being with great self-awareness. He was vulnerable, and he always struggled to become more spiritual. I immediately identified with him. He and I, as well as others in our faith community, were on a pilgrimage. He infused us with understanding and compassion. He showed us what it meant to say, "We are the Church." He helped us meet the needs of our hearts and empowered us to strengthen our faith.

Father Joe's homilies involved the analysis of a faith experience that very often paralleled one of my own. In addition to connecting through words, a silent communication and bonding occurred. Although he knew that everyone's pilgrimage had a personal dimension, he called upon all of us to be witnesses to one another and to share our common human struggle for purpose in life.

In his last homily, about two months before his death, at a parish church where he had been transferred, he talked about the themes of his past homilies. He stated that his most important message was that God is merciful, kind, compassionate, and forgiving. He is a God who does not demand perfection from us but calls us and empowers us toward perfection. God is not a vengeful being, concocted within the human mind and heart to mirror the theme of revenge and demand for punishment that is so strong in this world. God is not to be feared. God reaches out, not to punish us but to embrace us. In concluding his homily, he said, "I have been given the gift of faith and am embraced by the gift of God's love."

As Father Joe's death from cancer neared, a healing service was held for him and his community. At that service he again reaffirmed his relationship with each of us. As we embraced, he referred to our request to have him say our funeral Mass and said, "I'm sorry, Ralph, I won't be able to fill the bill."

Crying helped me to heal. At the wake, when people talked about how much Father Joe meant to them on their faith pilgrimages, I cried. At the funeral service, I cried. At the grave, I placed my hands on his coffin, said goodbye, and departed. I did not cry.

Father Joe's spiritual presence and guidance are still deeply felt by many of us. We continue to support one another's pilgrimage in a faith community, and help the needy whenever we can. My wife and I regard Father Joe's suffering and death as the culmination of his pilgrimage, as Christ's suffering and death were for Him. Father Joe's legacy to us as fellow pilgrims is to experience and render unto others the simplicity of love.

Ralph A. Bellas   *Normal, Illinois*

One in a Million Guided Her Back

My mother-in-law, Sadie, and her sister, Jean, were taken out of Catholic school in the late 1930s due to a scandal within her family. The parish priest at that time believed the story of the other party involved, even though Sadie's father had admitted guilt and begged forgiveness. My mother-in-law and her sister could not go back to the church or school again.

I married Sadie's son, John, in my parish church, and Sadie used to tell me very interesting stories.

She related that in one stage of her life she had ten schillings (fifty pence) to last her the entire week and she needed groceries. She was on her way to the shops to buy food, wondering how on earth she would manage.

Then, she told me, at that moment she passed by a bingo hall.

I thought, "Surely she didn't go in with very little food in the house!"

But she did and, behold, she came out with bags full of food enough to last two weeks. I hardly needed to ask why she took such a risk—by this time I already knew her Catholic background and how she would pray like mad for Our Lady to help her...as she did with the groceries!

The years went on and we had two sons. Our parish priest died and we got Father Michael, whom everyone loved. By the time our son Daniel was ready to make his first holy Communion, Sadie had started coming to the special Masses that were held in Dan's school.

One day Sadie asked me if I would get an appointment with Father Michael for her because she wanted to make her confession. Father Michael was so good to her; she said she felt like a queen. Father Michael was not only a parish priest but an entertainer as well. Oh, such a great man and priest!

He was then transferred to another parish, and the whole congregation was in tears. We went to Mass at his new parish a couple of times, as that was what Sadie wanted, but it was a good distance, and by now Sadie was seventy-four years old.

She had always been in poor health, but now she had cancer and knew it was time to die.

Sadie was home from the hospital for a few weeks, and every day that I went to her house I found her getting weaker and weaker. One day she asked if I had informed Father Michael of her illness. I told her that I had left a few messages but that he had a big church and hospitals to visit. Then, one Sunday I got a call from Father Michael saying he was going to be in the area and would pop in to see Sadie for a couple of minutes.

John, my husband, went down to tell his mother that Father Michael was going to see her. She was very weak and tired but when she heard that, she sat up, brushed her hair, and waited for him to arrive. When he walked into Sadie's room, she was so glad and proud he had called on her that her eyes lit up.

They had a bit of a chat, and he told her a joke and she laughed. He gave her a blessing and said he would pop back sometime.

Early the next morning, we got a phone call informing us that Sadie had died during the night, and in all honesty, we, her family, firmly believe she waited until Father Michael had called and blessed her. She had so much faith and love that she didn't want to die until she had been blessed by him.

Her recollection of parish priests from her childhood was so much different, but she loved Father Michael's devotion to the faith and his devotion to his people. As she said often enough, he was one in a million. He was amazed that she came back to the faith after sixty years, but I know it was Father Michael—the way he preached, his jokes and his caring—that guided her back

Pat A. Askew   *Gateshead, Tyne and Wear, England*

To Be Continued!

I met Father Anthony J. Lehmann, SJ, in the summer of 1982. Our daughter Lori was studying at Gonzaga University and was going abroad to Florence, Italy, for her junior year. Father Tony gave us parents the "do's and don'ts" about Florence, which was very beneficial to my wife and me, and to Lori. This meeting drew me to Father Tony and we were good friends until his death in 2002.

Father Tony baptized seven of our grandchildren, as well as our daughter and her husband and their sons at their home. He performed the sacrament of holy matrimony for our other daughter and her husband in 1989. He even baptized their two children in their Portland home when Gonzaga University played Portland at home and we went to the games.

Father Tony became like a member of our family. We all loved him so much. But it was not just our family—Father Tony was a member of many, many families. I believe he performed over a thousand marriages and baptized even more children.

He was never too busy to talk to you and give comfort if and when you needed it. Whenever we were in dire straits and needed prayers said for our special intentions, we would always call the Poor Clares and then call Father Tony. I really believe in the power of prayer, and this has been proven many times for us. I always thought that Father Tony was the ideal Jesuit and he proved it to me, my family, and many of our friends.

Since Father Tony passed away I have not ceased asking him to protect us. In the almost three years since his death, I have had several prayers answered that I credit to him. I continue to pray to him, "Father Tony, pray for us."

Father Tony would never say "goodbye" or "this is the end"…he would just say, "To be continued!"

Note from Sister Patricia: Father Tony spent the first part of his priesthood as a Carthusian monk in France. For almost twenty years in his quiet cell, he learned to pray and draw forth from God the great spiritual energy that allowed him to give to others seemingly without measure. Circumstances forced Father Tony's relocation from being a very isolated and holy monk to becoming a dynamic and active, yet equally holy, priest for the University of Gonzaga in Spokane, Washington. Often, Father Tony would offer Mass in our small Poor Clare chapel when we were in need—every time, as he would leave, he would lean over the railing and ask us to "pray to God that I pray well." It was his hidden life of prayer that always sustained him, since his life as a priest caused him always to be "on fire with the love of God for others."

Leonard F. Riley   *Spokane, Washington*

Enriching Our Faith

While I was wintering in south Texas in 1997, Bishop Roberto Gonzalez, bishop of Corpus Christi, said Mass one Sunday at the Sacred Heart Catholic Church in Rockport, Texas.

As I participated in Mass, I smelled the sweetest odor and kept looking around for evidence of incense burning.

"Surely," I thought, "I should be able to see the smoke rising."

The scent continued unlike any scent I had ever smelled. It was very strong but not overpowering, and I just loved it.

When I looked at the host the bishop raised, it began to glow.

"Gee, this is neat," I continued to think. "The bishop has some kind of bishop thing that turns on a little light behind the Host."

This was the first time I had ever seen a bishop do a Mass, so it was plausible to me.

After Mass, I asked a nun who was sitting next to me if they had burned incense during Mass. She replied that no incense had been burning, so I asked her if she smelled a sweet flower scent like roses, but again she said, "No."

I left Mass and thought about what had occurred all the way home. And I thought about it the rest of the day and evening. The next day I called a friend who had also been at the church and asked her if the bishop had something special that he put the Host in when he held it up at the consecration.

She said that she didn't know of any such device, and I then explained to her how I had seen the Host glow and had smelled roses all through the Mass.

Later I told Sister Nancy, who taught the Rite of Christian Initiation of Adults, and she said that the Blessed Mother had known that I was in discouragement and had given me a very special gift from Her.

I was extremely discouraged at this point in my life. I had been waiting nearly three years for an annulment so I could join the Catholic Church and receive Our Lord in the Eucharist.

My faith was truly enriched by this bishop who never knew of the gift I received. I wonder how many times that members of the priesthood, without ever knowing, participate in very special happenings that enrich our faith. I have often wished Bishop Gonzalez could be told of this wonderful gift I received at his Mass so that it might encourage him in his vocation.

Melva Gilbert   *North Manchester, Indiana*

Let's Pray

My husband had just returned from remote duty in Vietnam and Korea when our second son, John, was born with spina bifida. We were devastated because the doctors kept telling us he was not going to live very long. We had many important decisions to make before our move to my husband's next duty station within two weeks.

My husband remembered Father Stanley Powers, a priest at the Newman Center where we had gone to college. He called him and Father Powers came to the hospital that same day to pray with us, and to baptize and confirm John. After he left, he continued to check on us, and even wrote to us after we had moved. We knew we had a very special priest praying for us.

The doctors did not offer much hope that our son would survive. My husband and I spent days in the library trying to learn all we could, but we only became more confused and depressed. Out of frustration, one day we decided to get in our car and just drive. We didn't know where we were going; we just had to get away. After driving aimlessly for an hour, my husband spotted a Catholic church and suggested that we stop and talk to a priest.

We were on the east side of Tucson, Arizona, and I do not recall the name of the little church or the priest that came to the door. After telling him our story, I remember him saying, "Let's pray." His words expressed all the emotions we felt but did not know how to express. His prayer lifted all our worries to God, and we felt so much more at peace afterwards.

Father Stanley Powers and the priest who prayed with us at the church in Tucson taught us the power of prayer. Our son is now teaching science to emotionally disturbed children.

Jane M. Goetz   *San Antonio, Texas*

Father Would Not Let Me Go

Like many young people today, after graduating high school we seem to fall away from the church. For me, it was nearly fifteen years of sleeping in on weekends or finding some *resembled spirit* in California's Sierra Nevada Mountains, but it wasn't until 1991 that I renewed my faith and began my journey toward God as an adult.

Upon moving to Pittsburgh, Pennsylvania, I contacted St. Margaret of Scotland Parish. Father Francis Xavier Lackner answered my call, saying that the parish was over-crowded, but if I wanted to come I would be welcome. He was then in his 70s, and a man of great faith and love of God. He became my friend and my reason for rebuilding my Catholic faith.

Father's strength was abounding, and often he encouraged me not to give up hope. He listened to all my problems with an open mind and heart, always pleading for forgiveness on my part of those that hurt me, even if just imagined.

Father Lackner knew my travails, and prayed with me and for me with a sense of peace that I strived to attain. He knew my financial struggles and knew my efforts to get out of poverty, sometimes to no avail. He taught me respect of myself and what wholesome respect from men was.

Many thought him to be very strict and backwards, but this honorable man of God upheld the moral standards by which few abide. He respected marriage, and when I asked to attend the *widowed and divorced group*, he discouraged me because I had never actually been married. Many would have done it anyway, but I looked up to Father Lackner as a man of great wisdom in the light of the Holy Spirit.

He discouraged Communion to those who lived a less than pure lifestyle, but also knew they were children of God and that God loved them anyway, as we should love others like God does us. Less than pure lifestyles included promiscuity, revealing clothing for young women, drinking, drugs, sex before marriage (even for adults), vulgarity, gambling, gluttony, abortion, stem-cell research, cloning, and pedophilia behaviors.

Each week we learned everyday life issues and how to live our lives according to the word of God. Father helped us apply God's word to modern times. He taught me that every unborn child should have a name, and he taught me that every soul belongs to God no matter how life strays.

He taught me that everything we do affects our tomorrows and the day after and the day after that. And that what we do affects others. Through him, I learned to believe in the Holy Spirit and how to let the Holy Spirit into my life. I also learned that fighting makes matters worse, and anger is an open door to Satan. And I learned how to react differently when faced with distress.

He taught me how to pray, not just the Our Father or Hail Mary, but learning to connect with God in a full spiritual way and in turning my life and will over to the care of God. Father Lackner believed in me when I no longer believed in myself.

When I moved to Florida in October 1999, he was determined not to lose this soul he so heartily brought back to faith and God. I began working 80-90 hours a week that pulled me away from the church subtly and gradually, but Father would not let go. He sent me a card for Christmas 1999 in which he enclosed a small monetary gift.

It wasn't the money that made me register with a new local parish, it was his love of the poor, the needy, the helpless, the homeless, the striving, the disconnected, the separated, and the tormented—his love that wanted me to be a better person.

I am a better person because of Father Francis Xavier Lackner, and I pray that God has rewarded him immensely. I could not give back enough to him for what he gave to me: my life and love of the Lord.

Elaine M. Guglielmo   *Altamonte Springs, Florida*

Never Fear Pain and Suffering

Father John Henry Bush was the founding pastor of the Church of the Holy Family in Grand Blanc, Michigan. We first came to know him in 1957. To our family, he was not only our pastor, but a dear friend as well. He would show up unannounced at dinnertime, take a plate from the cupboard, and join our delighted parents at our family table. He did this with many of the families in the parish.

When we married in 1968, Stan and I began our own family and this tradition continued. Father Bush loved to share his faith with our children, and also a bit of mischief from time to time. He gave our eldest, Matt, his first mud bath and took him and his sisters on walks and bike rides, always bringing a bit of faith into the fun. Besides administering the sacraments to our children, he buried my beloved parents and saw us through some dark days.

Father Bush was never idle. He ran the parish and grade school. He walked daily and was always on the go until he was in his eighties. Even then he celebrated daily Mass with assistance, and was there for the six o'clock Mass most mornings. His poor health necessitated surgery on his heart, and what followed was perhaps the greatest witness of faith he ever gave to us.

In the late 1990s Father Bush underwent heart surgery. Around the same time, our family moved into a new home. Two months later, I received a phone call from him. He said, "Mary Jo, I owe you an apology. I wasn't able to get out to bless your new house but I will be there Sunday morning at eleven o'clock."

I was astounded that he knew we had moved, let alone was concerned about blessing our house. I had not seen Father Bush since his surgery, and I was amazed at how frail he was. Nonetheless, he insisted on blessing every single room. He went upstairs and downstairs, and then into the basement to get the furnace and sump pump, and even the foundation. The effort that this took was apparent.

When he was finally satisfied with the blessing and its explanation to our family, Father Bush gave in to his discomfort. Then came the words that I hope will stay with us all our lives. He said that he had never been in real pain before his surgery. During his stay in the hospital he had bouts of excruciating pain that became his greatest joy. He told us, "Don't fear pain and suffering. This is where you will encounter Jesus, just you and Him. Nothing else can distract you. You will be on Calvary with Him, and the joy is not possible to express. Your heart and His will beat as one."

What a testimony. Shortly thereafter, Father Bush passed away. We will remember him for many things: his humor, his love for his *bingo people*, his late night television catechism, pastoral direction, and qualities and stories too numerous to mention. But what we will remember most about Father John Bush is his love of his priesthood, his Church and his God.

Mary J. Byk   *Grand Blanc, Michigan*

Saved by Priestly Blessings

My two daughters, Madonna and Angela, traveled with me to Maryland in late May 2004 for the wedding of another daughter, Lisa. After having a nice family get together and visit we left to return home on Pentecost Sunday. Before leaving we attended Mass at Sacred Heart Catholic Church in Bowie, Maryland with my daughter Pat and her husband Bob.

After Mass, Pat introduced us to Msgr. Charles Parry, Father Tim McMorland, and Father Tappe. All of them blessed each one of us and our van. They were wonderful and caring priests.

As we headed down Highway 70 through Maringo, Indiana, that evening, we encountered six tornadoes. As I looked in the direction of the city, a tornado hit a transformer and the sky lit up. I turned around in my seat and witnessed a funnel cloud right behind our van. We were directly in the path of the potential twister. I yelled to my daughter Madonna, to step on the accelerator. Thanks be to God and the priests' blessings from Sacred Heart Catholic Church, we were saved from the funnel cloud.

In all my seventy-seven years, I have never experienced anything as scary as that moment. We will forever remember the kindness and blessings provided by those wonderful men of God. Never forget that blessings really do make a difference.

Elsie R. Herrmann   *Millstadt, Illinois*

Father Ed's Honesty

During Thanksgiving of 2004 I met Father Ed Hallinan at a teachers' retreat held for the faculty of my white, middle- to upper-class suburban Catholic school. He was the guest speaker and celebrant for the Liturgy.

Father Ed began his talk with a story from his seminary days at St. Charles Seminary in Overbrook, which is near Philadelphia, Pennsylvania. Before his first assignment at a parish, he asked his superiors if he could be assigned to an inner-city parish. He had been raised to have racist attitudes, which was more the result of ignorance than a deliberate intent to be unloving, and he wanted to be healed from this mindset. His superiors, who were surprised at the reason for his request, obliged him.

At this point in the talk I was truly amazed at Father Ed's honesty. This priest was being completely candid with us about a common fault of a certain generation of white, middle-class people. He had admitted to

206

himself, to his superiors, and to God that he was less than perfect in his attitudes towards people of different cultures, and he sincerely wanted to do something about it.

Father Ed's talk continued and he eventually spoke about his present assignment at St. Martin de Porres in Philadelphia. His parish school is one hundred percent African-American and many of the students do not belong to the Catholic faith, let alone St. Martin's Parish. These families truly sacrifice to send their children to a school that provides safety as well as high academic and moral standards.

In a completely selfless manner, Father Ed told us how very involved he is with the faculty, the students, and their families. He told us stories of how hard he works to get to know the family backgrounds of his students. We learned how he makes sure that an inability to pay tuition never compromises a student's education. He finds grants, people capable of making endowments, and any means necessary to ensure that his students are able to have the education they deserve and want.

He spoke of funny anecdotes, friendships he's made within his parish, and trying to make ends meet financially. We were also told of his doubts, his tiredness, and the effects a brutal pace as the pastor of more than one parish has had on him (Many Philadelphia parishes have merged or closed in the last thirty years). He also told us about the retreats he takes for spiritual refreshment.

Father Ed shared his stories in an honest and open manner, exposing his humanity within the context of his priesthood. He realizes God's hand at work in his life, and the more Father Ed spoke, the more amazed I became.

Jesus' message of peace and love was, and continues to be, for all people. The letter of His law is love. Father Ed, as an ordained priest of some twenty years, humbly embodies this message and this love.

Teresa M. Pietruch   *Reading, Pennsylvania*

Priests Are People Too

At first, I didn't think much of it that September morning in 2002 when my husband's first cousin, Father Jeevan D'Cunha, contacted us. I'd met him several years ago when I had visited India, and never expected to see him again. At that time he was still in the seminary in Bombay, and I remembered him as a very tall, timid, and docile sort of fellow.

Now he was studying here in the United States at Boston College, and was calling to say he wanted to spend his Christmas break with my family. That fall the priest scandal had broken out across the country, and I remember telling a friend when I was on retreat later that month how nervous I was about Father Jeevan coming to stay with us. I just didn't know what to expect.

Although we'd had lots of friends and relatives stay with us in the past, we never had a priest as a houseguest. My nervousness quickly turned into joy when Father Jeevan arrived. He was so friendly, funny, down-to-earth, and loving, especially with our four children. Before we knew it, we'd grown completely attached to him. In fact, we all missed him so much after he left that we couldn't wait for him to come back.

There were several *firsts* that took place in our home during that Christmas break. We had Mass in our home, he taught our boys to be altar servers, he heard their confessions, and he even went on a three-day trip with two other families and us. He played endlessly with the children in whatever games they chose.

By spending time with Father Jeevan, I, a mother of four, have learned to love a little bit better. I have also learned to remember that priests are people too. They need love, daily prayer, and nurturing just like everyone else. And my children learned that they could love their *uncle* and have a close friendship with someone who happens to be a priest.

Diana Farias, SFO   *Concord, California*

The Extra Mile

In the Archdiocese of Philadelphia, Pennsylvania, there are many wonderful priests and religious. But there is one special priest who really has gone the extra mile to educate, work with, encourage, and support his parishioners. He is Msgr. Gregory J. Parlante, the new pastor at Saint Cornelius Church in Chadds Ford, and former pastor at Holy Name of Jesus Parish in Philadelphia.

While at Holy Name of Jesus Parish from 1999 until 2004, Msgr. Parlante worked with his parishioners and encouraged them. He increased their liturgical as well as scriptural awareness, and fostered in so many a love for the Church and for God's people. Each week he spoke to his parishioners during the homily and told them how good they were and how much God loved them. There is nothing self-serving about him.

Msgr. Parlante also encouraged and fostered vocations to the priesthood and religious life, and invited his parishioners to look around at the young people to see who among them might have a religious vocation, and invite them to consider it. His great love for the prayer life and sacramental life of the Church made every occasion a time of profound beauty, deep prayer, and good liturgy. Monsignor also gave mini-retreats and workshops for the people, and these were always well attended. All who participated in his parish were prepared with such care and love.

His great sense of humor, his deep joy, and his solid life of prayer serve as an example to all who know him and love him. His solicitude is inclusive and extends beyond parish borders as well. A former director of vocations, Msgr. Parlante reaches out to men and women and invites them to listen and respond to God's call however they receive it. He makes himself available to his many friends and acquaintances for Masses, special occasions, talks and workshops.

Monsignor Parlante is a well-rounded man with a great sense for beauty, fine art, and the sacred in our daily lives. People usually feel better after being around him; he brings out the best in so many.

It is not every day you meet a priest who encourages you to know your faith and to realize how much God loves you, but Msgr. Parlante does just that. He does it in such a genuine way that you cannot help but feel a part of our beautiful faith-tradition. Priests like this need to be recognized, supported and encouraged, so that others like him may come to work with us, the people of God.

Sr. Colette M. Campellone, OSF   *Wilmington, Delaware*

It Is Impossible to Remain the Same

Nestled on the top of a mountain in the middle of wonderful nature is the village of Kozhaya in the Middle Eastern country of Lebanon. Here lies a small church where Father Antonios Chayna has lived as a hermit for about eighteen years. He is an exceptional priest and monk, especially in our days.

Father Antonios is a member of the Lebanese Maronites Order and is one of the rare hermits in the world. With seven PhD's, he worked with young people in many countries for a long time before returning to Lebanon where he worked very hard to gain the papal benediction to become a hermit.

Hundreds of people of all ages from around the world have visited and continue to visit Father Antonios every day to receive his guidance and blessings. When you visit him in this small country on the Mediterranean Sea, it's impossible to remain the same. He has truly changed the lives of many.

Father Antonios is a living example of how a Christian priest should be. He has sacrificed his entire life for all the sons of God. If you visit him, you will find him in his hermitage—an old man wearing black who prays night and day for you and me, living as a saint.

Victoria M. Chaina   *Barsa El-Koura, North Lebanon, Lebanon*

Who Am I?

I was raised in a devout Catholic family. My parents were involved in all the Christmas and summer fetes run by our parish, and we said the rosary together as a family at night. We attended Mass, confession, and other services like Benediction, and kept Fridays as days of fasting.

When I left school, I stopped going to Mass as many of my friends and elder brothers and sisters had done. I started looking at church-going people as hypocrites who were weak and ignorant. My life went on, and I felt nothing was missing. Perhaps this was because, despite having received my first sacraments and gone through the motions of being Catholic, our faith had never really touched me. Practicing my religion had never been a personal decision or commitment, and services seemed boring. They left me cold.

The priests I had known while I was growing up always appeared to be confident, forceful, and big men who, in a way, intimidated me. When they came to our home to visit I tried to stay out of their way. We young ones would make a dash for the stairs when a priest arrived, leaving the grown-ups to entertain alone. This way we felt we wouldn't have to own up to some failing or other.

Around 1995, after about fifteen years of not going to church except for an occasional midnight Mass, I was drawn back to it for some reason.

I attended a Mass at our local church, St. Elizabeth's, Peel Hall, which is in the northwest of England, in Manchester.

When I went to this particular Mass, I was astonished to hear the parish priest at the time, Father Tony, giving a homily that seemed to come right from his heart. It was about the successes and also (and to me more importantly) the struggles he'd experienced in the past. His words touched me deeply. I started going to Mass again, and each time I went I was amazed that this priest would speak to me. He sincerely showed concern when he asked me how I was.

Sometimes a few older parishioners were invited to the presbytery after Mass, and once or twice I went along too. One time Father Tony asked me who I am, and after I left him I began to think deeply about his thought-provoking question. Initially, I could only think of answers like, "I'm my parents' daughter, and so and so's sister" and could only define myself by where I'd gone to school and what my job was. As I pondered his question, though, I began to think about many things: like what my faith meant to me, and what my reasons were for decisions I had made throughout the years.

Father Tony was very gentle and accepting, and I think that's what first inspired me to learn more about our faith. For the first time, I was discovering for myself the riches of the Catholic Church, as well as my worth as a child of God. So you see, it's not always the confident people who seem to have all the answers, who touch people's hearts, and give them the desire to draw closer to God. It's also those who are struggling and facing all kinds of setbacks themselves who are Christ to us misfits and broken people.

Father Tony Elder will always have my respect and utter gratitude for how his quiet words of encouragement at a difficult time led me to a real and living faith in my God. To any priest who is worried or anxious, or of a quieter and less outgoing disposition, I want to thank you for hanging in there. Perhaps you'll have the opportunity to turn someone's life around too by simply being there for a stranger who pops into your church one day. I'm sure your reward will indeed be great in heaven.

Chris J. G. Austin   *Manchester, Greater Manchester, England*

I Needed to Return

In 1967, I married a non-Catholic. Walt allowed me to raise our children Catholic, but never considered becoming a Catholic himself. His dad was an atheist and his mom a German Lutheran, and they did not approve of Catholics.

Two and a half years ago, when we lost my mother, I started feeling that I needed to return to the Church of the Resurrection where I had received all of my sacraments. It was *home* to me. Walt didn't want me to go alone each week, so he went too.

A young priest at the church, Father Jeffery Robideau, really got through to Walt with his energetic and insightful homilies. Walt even went to church by himself when I couldn't due to illness. Although this priest did not celebrate every Mass at our church, Walt kept going back for more.

After about six months Walt told me it was time for him to become Catholic. He said he wanted all the benefits that come with being Catholic. Wow! I never thought it would happen. He spoke with Father Robideau and started private instructions with the priest and the man who would sponsor him. On April 10, 2004, Walt was baptized and confirmed, and after the Easter Vigil our dear Father Robideau married us in the Church.

During this time we became close friends with Father Robideau. He is the spiritual director of a Carmelite Community, and soon my husband and I started studying to become third order Discalced Carmelites. On May 17, 2004, my sister Debi, Walt, and I were clothed at our Carmelite formation.

Through Father Robideau we have met Carmelite sisters who live about an hour from our home. Debi, Walt, and I have *adopted* them and bring care packages to their monastery once a month. The Carmelite formation group also helps provide items that we give the sisters.

Walt's co-workers are amazed that during his breaks at work he pulls out prayer books and various other religious books to read. And recently he became an usher. Who would have ever thought that would happen? (Oh yeah, Father Robbie would have!)

Father Robideau was assigned to Jackson Prison to minister to the inmates and is no longer at our church. However, we keep in touch and continue to feel very blessed to have him in our lives. Father Robideau brought us very far in our spiritual lives. We can never thank him enough for all the peace we have received in the past few years.

Susan K. Newberry   *Lansing, Michigan*

A Word to the Wise

God bless all the priests who counsel the aged. Kindness, patience, consideration, and humor are certainly necessary!

After I retired, I had become very cozy in the routine of the Liturgy of the Hours and eucharistic adoration. I particularly enjoyed daily Mass because Father Mraz's daily sermons are outstanding with his insight into the daily liturgy, the historical background, and the impact of the saint of the day.

When I was seventy-five years old my husband had two consecutive surgeries. My daily Mass was out. With frustration and concern, I told Father Mraz of my dilemma. He quietly advised, "You are not a nun. You don't need to go to Mass every day. Go home and take care of your husband!"

Another crisis arose when I fell asleep for thirty-five minutes during my weekly eucharistic adoration hour, to which Father Mraz said,

"Saint Theresa always told her nuns, 'If you fall asleep during prayer, it is because you are TIRED!'"

Even the elderly need wise spiritual advice.

Mariann H. Otto   *Lester Prairie, Minnesota*

A Humble Warrior for God

As a deacon, I am obligated to have a spiritual advisor to assist me on my faith journey. Besides being a friend, Father Leo Charlebois (1910–1993) became that person during the 1980s. We shared many special moments as we regularly met once a month and at times when we concelebrated Mass.

Father Leo was a small, gentle person who had served in the Air Force, during World War II, as a flight engineer on the bombing runs in Europe. He told me that, when ever possible, he would visit the holy places and spend time reflecting. He said whenever they were to fly on a mission, the chaplain would meet him with the Eucharist just before he boarded his plane. His men felt secure when he flew with them. It was obvious that even before his ordination as a priest he was the light of Christ in the lives of those around him.

Father Leo was a humble person from a poor family in Quebec. After the war, he began his studies and entered the priesthood. He became a missionary in the Philippines but had to return home because of his sick mother. He then became an Air Force chaplain. A former military person myself (I had served in the army), I met many of his flock who truly loved him and what he represented to them and their families.

I guess we became close friends because he was a lover of St. Francis and I was a Third Order Franciscan for several years. Although gentle, he was a strong warrior for Christ. He influenced my approach to the

215

way I carry out my diaconate roll, the way I reach out to others, and the way I preach.

I remember one weekend I had preached about forgiveness towards persons that make those big mistakes, not just the every day little things. I mentioned it could be people we looked up to all our lives, a parent, a priest or some distinguished person in the community, and the act could have been anything from stealing to sexual abuse. Although I received many good comments about the homily—even two priests had favorable words for me—one person attacked me about mentioning priests and sexual abuse.

I mentioned this person's comments to Father Leo, and his comments were: "We are warriors for Christ. We must never avoid standing up as clergy and share his Cross for the good of the Church. Be thankful you were wounded for Jesus."

During the last years of his life his eyesight left him and he suffered from a blood disease, needing transfusions almost weekly near the end. Yet he continued to carry out his priestly commitments to the best of his ability, never complaining.

True humility, I am told, comes when, in the light of God, we have seen ourselves to be nothing, have consented to part with and cast away self, and have let God be all.

Father Leo was a humble warrior who learned, through his life experiences of serving, that by putting on the Lord Jesus he had put on the heart of compassion, kindness, humility, meekness, and long suffering. Jesus had taken the place of himself, and it was not impossible for him to forgive like Jesus forgave.

He never asked for more than he received but gave everything he had for the cross of Christ. My life and my ministry have been blessed by walking a part of the journey with him.

Deacon Lee Winchester   *Ottawa, Ontario, Canada*

My Friend, Confidant, and Confessor

Msgr. David W. Steinbrickner from Long Island, N.Y. was ordained and then remained in the Diocese of Ogdensburg, New York for his entire priesthood. He was my friend, confidant, and confessor for thirty years. He was Jesus to me—the true suffering Jesus.

David suffered from kidney failure, and after many hospitalizations he was placed on home-based dialysis. I watched this tall, dark-haired, handsome man work like a field hand, and still continue his four-hour regiment on the dialysis machine. During this time he was appointed to the seat of vicar general for two bishops.

This holy monsignor suffered terribly, but never complained. For eighteen years, while he was on dialysis, he worked hard in his garden so he could share food with the poor, and continued to fulfill all of his priestly duties. This is an amazing feat for a dialysis patient.

Two years before he died, Msgr. Steinbrickner received a kidney transplant, and his aged and ailing mother moved to be closer to him. Unfortunately, the transplant failed. Then his circulation failed, and he was wounded further when he lost his fingers, one at a time. I wrote for him and took care of him and I never heard him complain. At times he moaned in pain, and it was then that I was given the privilege of holding the suffering Jesus.

I watched as he concelebrated his last Mass for his mother from a bed that was wheeled onto the altar. My heart ached as he said the responses from his place on the sickbed. It was the same strong voice we all knew so well.

Before she died, I saw the monsignor's mother say her final good-byes to him with his stubs of hands in hers. Their eyes met, and she just shook her head up and down. There was acceptance in her heartache, and she, like her son, never complained. Dorthea went to be with Our Lord on July 29, 1979. David lived on in suffering until April 26 of the following year.

Stephen L. Henry   *Ogdensburg, New York*

A Single Mother

As a single mother of three young boys, times were very hard for us. It was 1981 and my sons were three, six, and eight years old. Nothing could describe the deep loneliness and pain I felt as I raised my sons in poverty while trying to be a good mother. We took solace in our parish community at St. Joseph Church in New London, Connecticut.

Since I did not have a car, we walked to church every day to attend daily Mass. It was there that I found peace. Soon our pastor, Father Joseph Castaldi, took my sons under his wing and became a wonderful role model for them. My two oldest sons became altar servers, and their job was to assist Father Castaldi every morning at Mass. Because of this very important commitment, they woke up early every morning before school to arrive at church on time.

Father Castaldi gave my sons jobs to do around the church and rewarded them by paying their tuition, which, as a single and very poor mother, I never could have afforded. He continued to support them throughout their years at St. Bernard High School.

My sons admired Father Castaldi so much when they were little that one morning, before the eight o'clock Mass, my middle son, Jason, took the scissors he had found in the sacristy and cut off all his hair to be bald like Father Castaldi. When the bell rang and they walked out to begin the Mass, I nearly died when I saw Jason's hair all cut off. Father Castaldi had been in the yard before Mass and did not see him do this.

When I asked Jason why he cut his hair off, he said, "To look more like Father Castaldi."

All year long we would shop for little gifts to put in a Christmas stocking that would become Father Castaldi's Christmas present from us. Early in our relationship, Father Castaldi told my boys that he had been poor as a child and didn't receive Christmas stockings. Then after eighth grade he went right into the seminary and didn't get a stocking there either. Our Christmas stocking project became very important to my sons because they wanted to give him all the stockings he had missed as a child. They used their few dollars from serving weddings to buy little gifts for his stocking, and wrapped each one with love.

When the boys got older and entered high school they worked part-time jobs and were on a mission to buy Father Castaldi a new chalice because the one he had been using was ceramic and had a crack in it. The three of them pooled their money to buy him a beautiful silver one and had it engraved: "To Father Castaldi from the Catala brothers."

Through his example, Father Castaldi showed my boys how important it is to celebrate the Eucharist, how important commitment is, and how loved and valued they are. He filled a void in their little hearts, and was a true father to them. He taught them everyday values and principles, and by allowing them to be in his life, he was a wonderful and powerful testament to his vocation to the holy priesthood.

Today, as a city councilor in the city of New London, my son Jason thinks with his heart. He listens to the people and hears their needs. He is the one called upon to open the council meeting with a different prayer each time they meet. Jason also reaches out to the students in his sixth-grade class, and helps all of them in times of need. He is such an outstanding teacher that Walmart named him "Teacher of the Year." Jason attributes his success to the fact that when he was young, someone cared and influenced him to be the man he is today. He told me once that he passes on what was given to him as a child by Father Castaldi. He is following closely in the footsteps of a truly holy man of God.

Father Joseph Castaldi's influence touched all three of my sons' lives very deeply. Today they are grown men and are still close to this incredible priest. They have all attended college, and are living successful lives.

Genevieve D. Catala   *New London, Connecticut*

The Traveling Priest

We called him "The Traveling Priest." Upon turning sixty-five years of age and officially retiring from diocesan ministry, Father Peter Hussey began to wander throughout our vast rural diocese. He drove a beat-up old car, going wherever the Holy Spirit and his brother priests called him to help.

Lay folks loved him, particularly teenagers and young adults who were struggling to remain faithful in today's world. It was not unusual for Father Hussey to show up in the strangest places and at the most unusual times: just when we were in need of a good confession, some spiritual counseling, or a convenient out from a situation involving peer pressure that threatened to lead us astray.

Father Hussey somehow remembered each of our names, even if he had only met us once. He simply showed up out of nowhere wearing a Roman collar and a black fedora, dangling the beaten beads of his wooden rosary from his fingertips.

During the summer between high school and college, I found myself spiritually adrift and hanging out with a crowd that was leading me away from the Catholic Church. Father Hussey found out about this situation, voiced his disapproval and invited me to visit Madonna House—a lay community in a neighboring diocese founded by a friend, Catherine de Huek.

"Nothing is more important in life than your soul," Father Hussey said, "And God only gave you one. Therefore, I cannot let you lose it."

Father Hussey knew what I needed to shore up my faith. I spent the days working on the farm or in the woods. During the evenings we would frequent Mass at the chapel, listen to spiritual teachings from the saints, and eat good, hearty food grown on the farm. My faith returned.

A day or so before I was scheduled to return home, the car in which I was traveling broke down. I panicked. My parents were away that weekend and I did not have sufficient cash on hand for a bus ticket home. Moreover, there was no bank nearby where I could withdraw sufficient funds.

I was frantic, but the people of Madonna House were quite understanding. They urged me to pray. I had a rosary in my pocket that Father Hussey had blessed before I left for Madonna House. But I found prayer difficult because I was angry at God for abandoning me after I had come here on faith that He was acting through Father Hussey.

The afternoon I had been scheduled to leave, I found myself working in the business office across from the main hall. Despite my best efforts, I spent more time panicking than praying. We were just ready to break for afternoon tea when a dusty brown car pulled up across the road. It seemed strangely familiar for some reason.

Out popped an elderly priest holding an old wooden rosary in one of his hands. His other hand reached back into the car for a black hat.

"Father Hussey!" I cried as my former doubts evaporated.

"Peter," smiled the old priest. "I was just passing by when I felt the urge to stop for a visit. I'm so glad you decided to visit this place. Has it helped strengthen you in the faith?"

As we drove home that evening, I shared with Father just how much the visit to Madonna House really had strengthened my faith. I then thanked him for his timely advice that had kept me from wandering further away from the Faith. We then prayed a rosary before stopping at a friend's house for a bite to eat.

Although Our Lord has since called Father home, I still visit Madonna House whenever the opportunity arises. And with each visit, I pray for Father Hussey, the traveling priest. I also pray that God may send us other priests who share Father Hussey's love of the Church and zeal for souls.

Pete Vere   *Nokomis, Florida*

Pete Vere, JCL, is a lay canon lawyer and the author of *Surprised by Canon Law: 150 Questions Catholics Ask About Canon Law.*

Bless Me Father

From my earliest years I always wanted to be a priest. At times the desire became a bit diminished, but after may trials, I am a priest. For all eternity I am a priest! Why is this important to me? The reasons are many and profound. Let me give you one.

The number of *confessions* are down these days. Many among us have lost the sense of sin and the need for forgiveness. As a result, a priest spends much time in the confessional without accomplishing very much. Yes! The humble Catholics still come and confess their peccadilloes. Thank God for these good Catholics.

But every now and then a quiet voice whispers: "Bless me Father for I have sinned. It has been ten years (or twenty or thirty or even fifty-five) since my last confession."

Whenever a priest hears confessions, he always forgives sins, "acting in the person of Jesus Christ, the Great High Priest." But in these moving moments, the priest really feels the power of the priesthood. In these memorable moments of mercy, the Father of the Confessional puts on the mantle of the merciful and forgiving Lord.

Imagine! The priest has the power, directly from Jesus Christ, to forgive every sin under heaven. No matter how vile! No matter how many! When these moments come in the confessional, I thank God for my vocation.

Could someone else have done as well, if not better than myself. Yes! Without a doubt. But someone had to be there to answer that *quiet voice*. I was that someone who responded to that call for mercy and forgiveness. In these moments, more than ever, I thank God for my vocation.

Yes, my dear young men, become priests! At times, the waters are turbulent, as they are these days. But the Lord is always with us. He never abandons His priests! Remember when Jesus was accosted by the arresting soldiers in the Garden of Olives, He stood firm against His accusers: "If you seek me, let these men go." Jesus always takes care of us poor weak human priests. Come in! The water is fine!

Fr. Richard J. Rego, STL   *Ajo, Arizona*

What a Gift

Today I look back over fifty years as a Franciscan priest and can hardly believe it! I, whom many people thought wouldn't last in the post-graduate seminary, "…because he had too many girl friends in high school!" Yet, here I am, fifty years later! How did I do it? God overcame great obstacles and penetrated my thick skull.

I owe my vocation to the overpowering grace of God. He knocked Paul off his horse, but was gentler with this Irishman. He chose the channel of my saintly Irish mother, who prayed for this vocational gift for me. Her brother, a Jesuit priest, was surely influential in my life as was our Redemptorist pastor. By this and other means, our Good Lord enticed me to follow Him and share in His priesthood.

What a gift! To be allowed to feed His people, as He did, but with His Sacred Body and Precious Blood; to give birth to new life in God through the saving waters of Baptism, as when He stood in the river Jordan; in and through His forgiveness, to raise people from the death of sin; to bring His comforting love to sorrowing people and gently reassure them of God's love for them—no matter what; to witness the committing love of matrimony and rejoice in the feast, as He did; and finally, to weep with those experiencing the death of a loved one, as He wept for Lazarus. I know well that I am not worthy of such a gift.

A few words from a poem by George Herbert express this for me: "Love bade me welcome; yet my soul drew back…Quick-eyed Love… sweetly questioned, if I lacked anything? A guest, I answered, 'worthy to be here'; Love said, 'you shall be he!'"

I am eternally grateful for this wonderful, undeserved gift of God to me, in His priesthood! What a gift!

Fr. Maurus Kelly, OFM   *Santa Barbara, California*

The Hand of the Lord

In 1998 my father, Karl Rambossek, an Austrian immigrant to the United States, had a heart attack and was put on life support in the CICU at Exempla Lutheran Hospital in WheatRidge, Colorado. He was kept in a drug-induced coma to prevent his suffering and for nine long days our family prayed and agonized over what to do. The doctors were very clear with us that his heart was no longer capable of fulfilling its job.

My dad had heart disease, emphysema, and liver disease. He was seventy-one years old and not considered a good candidate for a heart transplant. We did not have many options. One thing we knew we wanted and that was to speak with a priest and ask his guidance.

We initially wanted to speak with Father Goggins, the rector of SS. Peter and Paul Catholic Church in WheatRidge, where my mom has been a parishioner since the early 1960s and where both my sister and I were baptized and married. However, he was not available at the time. The church did have a group of missionary priests staying there and the church secretary said she would be happy to have one of them come to the hospital to visit with us and say a rosary for Dad.

Sad to say, I cannot remember this priest's name, but he made a lasting impression upon me and my family. When he arrived, we greeted Father and began to explain the situation to him. Even though Dad was in a coma, we continuously kept his favorite music playing softly in the background to comfort and soothe him: Mozart, Strauss and Andrea Bocelli. The missionary priest said that he recognized the music as some of his own favorites and was so loving and God-giving that we felt comfortable with him right away and started sharing Dad's story.

My dad was born in the small village of Lilienfeld, Austria, in January of 1927. He grew up in the beautiful hills surrounding Lilienfeld and became a skilled and graceful artist. His artwork beautifies our homes and the homes of many of our good friends. We are forever grateful he left this legacy for us and his grandchildren. One of my most precious earthly possessions is a picture he created of himself as a boy, resting near a small brook in the Lilienfeld hills, his face turned to the heavens, a soft morning light glowing through the trees.

Dad spent his youth exploring the surrounding mountains and the village of Lilienfeld. He caught trout by hand in the creek running through the town and watched the trains as they lumbered in and out of the small train station there. His youth was filled with the happiness of a young child who found God's wonder everywhere he gazed.

Now as we gathered around Dad's hospital bed, monitors humming in the background, the respirator gently rising and falling providing Dad his life-giving oxygen, this loving priest listened with a smile and an open heart to all of our stories of our father. When we reached the part about his growing up in Austria, Father asked where, explaining that he had recently been to Austria and was enamored of the country. The minute we said Lilienfeld, Father's eyes lit up and he said, "I was just there!"

He bent over to my dad and described the books in the monastery at Lilienfeld, the abbey and its many glorious types of architecture, and, of course, the gentle green hills where my dad had grown up and played as a child. He bragged about Lilienfeld's uniqueness and told my dad that it was one of his favorite places on God's earth.

My mother, sister, and I were stunned. Clearly, God had sent this wonderful priest to us to reassure and to confirm that He is always watching out for us and is always with us. Although Lilienfeld is a very small community in Austria and very few people, let alone a priest in the United

States, are familiar with it, God had sent this special priest who had just been there to comfort us in our time of need.

Together we held hands around Dad's bed, saying prayers and reciting the rosary. Our eyes were filled with tears but we smiled at God's handiwork and thanked Him for this gracious gift.

A couple of days later we let Dad go to Jesus. We knew that God was waiting for him and that He would talk with Dad about Lilienfeld and the precious memories he once shared with us.

It has been six years since my Dad passed on. I think of this special priest often and marvel at the wisdom of our God who sent him to us.

Our God chose to use one of his priests to comfort us, to console us, and to remind us that He is everywhere and He always meets our needs. "The hand of the Lord feeds us; he answers all our needs." Psalm 145.

Cynthia I. Goehring   *Lafayette, Colorado*

Passing the Bar

All of the Oblates of the Virgin Mary (OMV) priests and brothers are inspirational, courageous men of faith. As the cantor at the St. Francis Chapel in Boston, Maryland, I have had the pleasure to get to know many of the priests on a spiritual and personal level. Although there are so many truly inspirational men among them, I would have to say that Father Tom Carzon, the director of the St. Francis Chapel, is my inspiration. Father Tom is an amazing, caring priest and on more than one occasion his words of wisdom, encouragement, and faith have seen me through some difficult times.

I graduated from law school in May 2004 and had taken the bar to become licensed as an attorney in July 2004. In November 2004 the results were on the way to each applicant. I had just walked into my apartment with the results envelope in my hand when the phone rang. I saw on the caller ID that it was from the St. Francis Chapel.

What perfect timing. I had planned on opening my letter with my friend Heather, who had also taken the bar with me, but with the reality of having the envelope in my hand, there was no way I would be able to wait for her to get her results the next day.

Father Tom asked how I was doing knowing that the results were due any day. I told him that I had the envelope in my hand and was trying to figure out what I should do: wait and open it with Heather on the beach the next day as we had planned or open it immediately.

Father Tom said I could go over to the chapel and open the letter with him if it would help to have someone with me. I agreed that I couldn't wait until the next day to open it and that it would be best to have someone with me in the event the results were not so good.

So with my envelope in hand I headed over to the chapel. Upon my arrival, I walked into the office where Father Tom waited. In the elapsed time of about twenty minutes he had purchased a beautiful *hope* rose, a box of chocolates, had on the internet a picture of St. Thomas More (the patron saint of lawyers), and thankfully, a box of tissues. Talk about having all the right stuff necessary to make the best of a stressful situation.

Upon opening the letter and reading those first couple of words, I knew I had been unsuccessful in my first attempt at the bar. As the tears came, Father Tom gave me a minute to process the results, then with his amazing ability of knowing the right words to say, offered a prayer for me that I would have the grace, strength, and most of all, faith to see God's will in the results as not necessarily negative but positive.

Eventually I did see the positive, and trusting in God's will, I decided to attempt the bar again.

As I sit here studying for a second time, I treasure the fact that I have had the opportunity to meet not only Father Tom, but all the OMV priests and brothers. Every last one of them has offered me their prayers, support, guidance, and inspiration. I am not only a better person because of them, but my faith has grown in ways I never imagined. It gives me great pleasure to know that I have been blessed to have such wonderful, inspirational priests in the Boston area.

My little postscript: I know that prayers are answered. In early May I received the news that I passed the bar exam thanks to Father Tom and all who prayed for me.

Rebecca L. Martin   *Boston, Massachusetts*

Boyfriend was of Another Faith

Chasity, my daughter, was a college student at the University of Michigan in Ann Arbor, Michigan. At that time she was also a member of St. Mary's Student Parish where the Rev. Thomas Firestone was the Pastor.

One day in one of his homilies on Sunday morning, Father Tom made the statement, "If what you have is better than what your future husband or wife has for their present faith, why wouldn't you convince or try to convince that person to your faith?" He continued by explaining that "God may be using you as an instrument of God's holy will to bring this person into a deeper faith experience."

"If you know that what you have is better than what they have, why not want them to convert for you?" A lot of people say, "I don't want my boyfriend or girlfriend to convert just for me!" Father said, "Why not? If you know that what you have is better, why not?"

Chasity said that she will never forget what Father Tom said in that homily about dating someone of another faith. It made a lot of sense to her. If you know that what you have is better than what they have, why wouldn't you want them to convert?

Chasity is now dating someone who is of the Anglican faith. Because Father Tom's sermon had made such an impression on her, she asked her boyfriend to convert to her faith. He said, "Yes!"

Lou Therese T. Anthony   *Flint, Michigan*

Authors by Location

Australia
Fr. Edwin Agius, MSSP, *Parkville, Victoria, 43, 65*

Canada
Alberta
Janet P. MacLellan, *Edmonton, 138*
Pauline T. Saretsky, *Ashmont, 167*

British Columbia
Shirley A. Archambault, *New Westminster, 100*
Joan A. Pogson, *Saanichton, 50*

Ontario
Christine M. Labrosse, *Gloucester, 12*
Sandy E. Whalen, *Kingston, 174*
Lorraine M. Williams, *Markham, 150*
Deacon Lee Winchester, *Ottawa, 215*

Nova Scotia
Corinne M. Quinlan, *Dartmouth, 124*

England
Pat A. Askew, *Tyne & Wear, Gateshead, 196*
Chris J. G. Austin, *Manchester, Greater Manchester, 211*
Freya Marshall, *Chatham, Kent, 88*
Fiona M. Owen, *Merseyside, 23*

Lebanon
Victoria M. Chaina, *Barsa El-Koura, North Lebanon, 210*

Philippines
Josephine R. Mata, *Quezon City, 77*

Scotland
Maria V. Bartlett, *Kinross, Tayside, 84*

United States of America
Arizona
Fr. Richard J. Rego, STL, *Ajo, 222*
Sharon E. Reidy, *Cottonwood, 158*

California
Phillip J. Campbell, *Roseville, 97*
Diana Farias, SFO, *Concord, 208*
Debbie A. Greco, *Manteca, 121*
Fr. Maurus Kelly, OFM, *Santa Barbara, 223*
Alicia L. Marquez, *Indio, 44*
Wendy M. Posh, *Covina, 130*
Josephine M. Shryock, *Woodland, 78*
Carolyn D. Susin, *Martinez, 99*

Colorado
Cynthia I. Goehring, *Lafayette, 224*
Emily L. Westover, *Centennial, 191*

Connecticut
Anne B. Caron, *Hartford, 118*
Genevieve D. Catala, *New London, 218*
Larraine C. Kennedy, *Stafford Springs, 189*
Louis B. Remlin, *Westport, 184*

Delaware
Sr. Colette M. Campellone, OSF, *Wilmington, 209*

Florida
Clare C. Andriello-Trosclair, *Palm Beach Gardens, 103*
Sr. Janet I. Cavilia, *Fort Lauderdale. 140*
Br. Mark E. DeBrizzi, *Venice, 163*
Elaine M. Guglielmo, *Altamonte Springs, 202*
Mary Maguire, *West Palm Beach, 52*
Lesley M. Vaitekunas, *Coconut Creek, 14*
Pete Vere, *Nokomis, 220*
Ruthann P. Weinstein, *Cape Coral, 173*

Georgia
Debbie B. Oliver, *Valdosta, 105*
Robby L. Strozier, *Macon, 26*

Illinois
Ralph A. Bellas, *Normal, 195*
Mary Jane Davis, *Frederick, 70*
Jennifer L. Garrity, *Chicago, 183, 192*
Susan E. Gorski, *Naperville, 101*
Jean M. Heimann, *Chillicothe, 134, 178*
Elsi R. Herrmann, *Millstadt, 205*
Gloria J. Huerta, *Wheaton, 188*
Jacqueline M. Leo, *Palatine, 94*
Mary Lou Schuster, *Joliet, 181*
Loretta M. Trentanelli, *Aurora, 19*

Indiana
Bonnie L. Born, *Terre Haute, 104*
Melva Gilbert, *North Manchester, 199*
Linda Pitcher, *Indianapolis, 91*
Remo J. Tonelli, *Lowell, 137*

Kansas
Rev. Michael Peltzer, *Harper, 113*
Annette Sosa, *Hugoton, 40*
Janice Strait, *Salina, 28*

Louisiana
Debra R. Fusilier, *Rayne, 80*
Sr. RoseMary Wessel, MSC, *Metairie, 156*

Index

A

accidents
 car catches fire, 104–105
 girlfriend recovers following prayer, 83–84
 paralyzed son recovers, 186–187
 potential twister avoided, 205–206
addiction to gambling, 148–150
Agius, Father Edwin, MSSP
 "His Only Desire" (Agius), 43–44
 "A Miracle Baby" (Agius), 65–66
Alfred, Father, 33
Aline, Sister, 139
"Always a Part of the Family" (Cavilia), 140
Andretta, Connie, 68–69
Andriello-Trosclair, Clare C., 103
angels
 deliver Eucharist to dying man, 156–157
 "My Guardian Angel" (West), 154–155
 "Two Guardian Angels" (Born), 104–105
anointing of the sick. *See also* death
 five weeks of life after, 138–139
 of grandson Edward by Father Sal, 126–128
 by the great physician Himself, 163–165
 healing after, 66–67, 139
 "A Peaceful Anointing" (Hoffman), 21–22
 spiritual health resulting from, 163–165
annulments, help with, 78–81, 179–180, 199–200. *See also* marriage
Anthony, Father, 128–129
Anthony, Lou Therese T., 228
"The Apology" (Pitstick), 58–59
Archambault, Shirley A., 100
Art, Father, 37
Ashbaugh, Father Bill, 148–150
Askew, Pat A., 196–197
Asselin, Jason, 143
Austin, Chris J. G., 211–212

B

Bagan, Father Philip, 33
baptism, 65–66

Bartlett, Maria V., 84–85
Baska, Father Patrick, 139
Bedard, Father Bob, 12–14
Bede, Sister, 116–117
Beidelman, Father Patrick, 91–93
Beiruit, Lebanon, 86–88
Bell, Father, 96–97
Bellas, Ralph A., 193–195
Bergener, Carol, 186–187
Bertagnoli, Cynthia A., 176–177
Berube, Father Louis D., 170–171
Bible study, 94–95
Blackburn, Father Michael G., OFM, 74–75
Blanchfield, Father, 174–175
"Bless me Father" (Rego), 222–223
blessings
 "He Blessed the Creek" (Bergener), 186–187
 the new house, 204–205
 "Saved by Priestly Blessing" (Herrmann), 205–206
Boll, Father John, 79–80
Bomba, Father Paul, 80–81
Born, Bonnie L., 104–105
Bory, Father Richard, 172–173
Botschka, John and Helen, 46
"Boyfriend was of Another Faith" (Anthony), 228
Breen, Father Joe Pat, 166
Breindel, Charles L., 86–88
Brooks, Father Jeddie, 105
"Building a Happy Family" (O'Connell), 145
Burbidge, Bishop Michael, 142
Bush, Father John Henry, 204–205
Byk, Mary J., 204–205

C

Campbell, Phillip J., 97
Campellone, Sister Colette M., OSF, 209–210
Caplis, Father Roger, 183
Carmelites, 213–214
Caron, Anne B., 118
Carzon, Father Tom, 226–228
Casnovsky, Dennis J., 3
Castaldi, Father Joseph, 218–219
Catala, Genevieve D., 218–219
Catholics, charismatic, 14–16

INDEX

INDEX

S

Saint Therese of Lisieux, 16–19, 172–173
Sal, Father, 126–128
Saretsky, Pauline T., 167–168
"Saved by Priestly Blessing" (Herrmann), 205–206
Schafer, Gina Marie, 155–156
Schmuck, Virginia, 106–107
Schneider, Father Ron, 46
Scholerman, Lucy, 61–62
Schuster, Mary Lou, 181–182
Schweska, John Joseph D., 9–11
Scott, Father John, 33
Sebastian, Father, 172–173
"Secret Mass in the School" (Mata), 77
"Secret to Finding Time" (Smith), 8
Sedlacek, Father Richard, 32–33
sexual abuse in the church, 146, 189
"Shower Curtain Confession" (McCarthy), 24–26
Shryock, Josephine M., 78–80
Sidel, Father George, 33
silent retreat, 150–151
Simbala School, Zimbabwe, 2
"A Simple Invitation" (Douglas), 116–117
"A Single Mother" (Catala), 218–219
"Sinners, Our Biggest" (Huerta), 188
"Sitting with Jesus" (Kennedy), 189
Skylstad, Bishop William S., 1–3, 32–33
Smith, Janet L., 146–147
Smith, Lois M., 8
"Something Good Is Going to Happen" (Sosa), 40–42
Sonnenberg, Mark, 74–75
sorrow
    "Healed of a Hidden Sorrow" (Owen), 23
    "In My Time of Sorrow" (Counter), 187–188
Sosa, Annette, 40–42
"A Special Anointing" (MacLellan), 138–139
"A Special Mass" (Andriello-Trosclair), 103
"A Special Priest" (Iida), 168–169
Spethman, Amanda L., 4–6
spiritual directors. See also role models
    Ashbaugh, Father Bill, 148–150
    Beidelman, Father Patrick, 91–93
    Charlebois, Father Leo, 215–216
    Connelly, Father Paul, 88–91
    Donachie, Monsignor Benjamin, 84–85

spiritual directors (continued)
    Gerardo, Padre, 44–45
    Kelly, Father Joe, 193–195
    Robideau, Father Jeffrey, 213–214
St. James-Pfouts, June R., 119–121
St. Martin's College, 32–33
St. Pius X Church, 1–2
Stechschulte, Lisa A., 148–150
Steinbach, Douglas R., 62–63
Steinbach, Jeanette F., 63–64
Steinbrickner, Monsignor David W., 217–218
"Stop! Someone Needs You!" (Ellertson), 48–50
Strait, Janice, 28
Strozier, Robby L., 26–27
suicide, 91–93
Sullivan, Father Patrick, 130–131
Susin, Carolyn D., 99

T

Tappe, Father, 205–206
Thompson, Father Mel, 191
Thomson, Deacon Bob, 125–126
"Three Priests" (Schmuck), 106–107
"To Be Continued!" (Riley), 198–199
Tom, Father, 188
Tonelli, Remo J., 137–138
Traczyk, Chaplain (Chaplain Tragic), 53–55
"The Traveling Priest" (Vere), 220–221
Travers, Father Vincent, 100
Treml, Father, 3
Trentanelli, Loretta M., 19–21
"A True Friend" (Posh), 130–131
Turner, Craig C., 56–57
"Twice Blessed" (Garrity), 192–193
"Two Guardian Angels" (Born), 104–105

U

university students guided by
    Lorei, Monsignor Louis, 9–11
    monastic community at St. Martins, 32–33
    Pfeffer, Father Chuck, 4–6
"The Unknown Priest" (Williams), 150–151

V

Vaitekunas, Lesley M., 14–16
Van Ommeren, Monsignor William, 6–7
Vance, Father Leslie, 8

B-9

INDEX

Vandenberg, Father Tom, 136
Vere, Pete, 220–221
Vincent, Father, 100
vocation
   advice of Monsignor O'Connor, 58
   "The Apology" (Pitstick), 58–59
   begins in the heart of the mother,
     56–57, 172–173
   Bishop Michael Burbidge's, 142
   call to the secular Franciscan Order,
     96–97
   family, role in encouraging, 143–144,
     223–224
   fasting and prayer, role in
     encouraging, 143–144
   "Finding My Vocation in Beirut"
     (Breindel), 86–88
   the gift of, 223–224
   Herlocker, Father Brian's, 144
   Jason Asselin's, 143
   Kelly, Father Maurus', 223–224
   Mastey, Father Gregory's, 142–143
   McCloskey, Father C. John's, 143
   Mode, Father Daniel's call, 56–57
   "My Conversion" (Saretsky), 167–168
   "My Reflections on Priesthood"
     (Skylstad), 1–3
   "Our God Is an Awesome God"
     (Morales), 29–32
   power of a mother's prayers, 56–57,
     223–224
   prayer and fasting, role in
     encouraging, 143–144
   priests role in encouraging, 142–143,
     223–224
   Richter, Father Thomas', 142
   saying yes to, 141–145, 222–223
   "A True Friend" (Posh), 130–131
   Williams, Father Peter's, 144

W

"Walking With Us" (Mulrooney), 47–48
"A Warm and Welcoming Church"
  (Hanley), 166
"We Have Seen Jesus" (Davis), 70–72
Weinstein, Ruthann P., 173–174
Welsh, Father William P., 94–95
Wessel, Sister RoseMary, MSC, 156–
  157
West, LaVern I., 154–155
Westover, Emily L., 191
Whalen, Sandy E., 174–175
"What a Gift" (Kelly), 223–224
"What Can I Do For You" (King), 55–56

"What If?" (Falzone), 96–97
Whealen, Father Martin, 191
White, Francis R., 115
"Who Am I?" (Austin), 211–212
Williams, Father Joseph, 144
Williams, Father Peter, 144
Williams, Lorraine M., 150–151
Wilson, Father Tom, 143
Winchester, Deacon Lee, 215–216
"A Witness of Grace" (Campbell), 97
Wolf, Patricia, SFO, 82
Woodard, Brother Aelred, 33
"A Word to the Wise" (Otto), 214–215

Y

"You Must Take Christ With You"
  (Couser), 153
"You're Going To Hell" (Trentanelli),
  19–21

Z

Zeck, Father George, 34–35
Zerr, Father Gary, 61–64
Zimbabwe, Simbala School, 2
Zirchelback, Father Ivo, 106–107